Finding Jane
Dealing With Child Abuse

Brenda Secor

Praise for Finding Jane

"Brenda's story underlines the importance of resilience and the value of support from those who believe in you. A must read for anyone who works with or hopes to work with children and youth at risk."

Eleanor Casey MSW, RSW
Community Counselor

"Finding Jane is a true and candid story of the strength of a child who faced the most difficult and violent of circumstances in her young life. It illustrates true bravery on the part of these children as well as the absolute necessity for a system with professionals who are able and willing to help a child in need. Brenda's story is truly an inspiration for other victims of childhood abuse to seek help, and should be a required reading for all those wishing to pursue a career/studies related to social justice."

Shannon Parsons
Research Coordinator
Victims of Violence Canadian Centre for Missing Children

"This is one book that counselors, teachers, guidance counselors, judges and anyone related to dealing with CAS (Children's Aid Society) and the court system should read to learn first-hand what can happen if you don't fight back. As for Jane she must be a special person and Finding Jane: well let's say you found each other."

Fran Lewis
Radio Talk Show Host

"Finding Jane offers my clients hope and light at the end of a broken system."

Denise Lamb, CYW
Senior Counselor
Kingston Youth Shelter

"I share excerpts from this book with students in the Child Abuse, Neglect and Family Violence course. Brenda poignantly brings to life the complexity of the issues involved in child abuse and its impacts on the victim. Brenda's story is also a source of inspiration to survivors, reminding them of the powerful resilience of the human spirit to overcome incredible adversity."

Cathy Waite, MSW, RSW
Child & Youth Worker Professor

"An incredible story of strength and resilience, that not only gives purpose and hope to survivors of childhood abuse and trauma, but to the CYW's (Child and Youth Workers) who are working with them. A must read for any child welfare worker."

Kim Ducharme, CCW, BA(CYC), CYC(Cert.)
Professor, CYW Program
School of Health & Community Services

"I have finished reading your book again and I still love it. Even though I know the ending I still kind of hold my breath wondering what will happen. You are an amazing woman, you were an amazing kid too, and I am full of admiration for you."

Love Jane

"...the anguish that comes with the stories of children involved in the child welfare system can easily wear on workers. This incredible story of strength and resilience restores hope and purpose."

Colleen McAlister Lacombe, SSW
Professor Child and Youth Worker Program

DEDICATION

This book is written for my family, whose support means the world to me. Also a thank you to Jane. Without you I may never have had a story to tell.

CONTENTS

Please note: where necessary
names and locations have been
changed to protect the privacy
of those involved.

ACKNOWLEDGEMENTS

Thank you to Jane who laboured over this project and provided insight. To this day her faith in me has been unwavering. Something I will be forever grateful for.

Also a big thank you to my husband and children whose love and support gave me the strength to see this book through to completion.

Peter Duffin deserves a huge thanks for providing editing, proof reading, and research assistance in the process of producing this book.

Finally another big thank you to my dear friend Tammy AuCoin. She took it upon herself to design my book cover. She also set up the www.findingjane.ca website.

INTRODUCTION

At times it is difficult to remember what a long, very long journey it has been. You see, I have had this story to tell for quite some time now. But it has never felt like the time was right to unearth memories of a past that in a lot of respects is best forgotten. If only things were that easy.

But as I sit here on my back deck appreciating nature's beauty, and the friends and family I now have, I realize finding the strength to tell my story is an absolute must.

I can say that I have been here before only to stumble, give up, and not proceed. Do I start at the beginning; do I reveal all? And if I do reveal all, will I be able to convey my true emotions without those emotions hindering my ability to tell my whole story?

True, one of the things I learned at an early age was that if I were going to survive I would have to shut down my emotions. Otherwise, those who were torturing and tormenting me at the time would win. And allowing them to win, even at a young age, was never my intention.

To them, I especially say, you need to be held to account; this story needs to be told. And just as importantly, it needs to be told for the sake of those who have been victims of child abuse, many of whom still harbour the psychological scars inflicted on them by their tormentors.

So here I am before you writing a book about dealing with the past, moving forward and building the life that I envisioned. I spent many years trying to forget my past for very good reasons. These memories overwhelmed me during an extended period of depression that I struggled through. Looking back this may have been the beginning of the healing process. There was a time when I felt certain that happiness would always elude me, or that I wouldn't recognize it if it showed up. Although the process was painfully slow I'm grateful that I continued to stay true to my path.

I was born in Kingston, Ontario in 1965 to a single alcoholic mother. I do try to keep in mind that her childhood was probably a nightmare. As a mother I have tried to make a better life for my children, and perhaps she was a better mother to me than her mother was to her.

I'm not saying that I was a perfect mother, far from it, but I was better than my mother and since that is what I have to use as a yard stick, I was a success. I have made lots of mistakes, but I love my children more than anything in the world. It is also my hope that my children will do better for their children.

Let me begin my story by saying that there are certain types of men who are attracted to alcoholic single women, and of course they are not men of honour. Unfortunately it makes perfect sense why pedophiles are attracted to these types of women – what better target than a child who has already been emotionally and physically abused by someone who then passes out cold for hours after their daily drinking binge?

I remember coming home from school and finding my mother passed out on the couch from overdosing on her various medications. When the police arrived they gave me the choice of staying with my mother, who doesn't look like she's going to live through this one, or going with my mother's partner, the pedophile. What a choice! And unfortunately staying with my mother seemed to be the greater of two evils. I remember leaving with her boyfriend, sure I didn't want to be with him, but scared that my mother would be dead in hours and I had nowhere else to go.

I've barely begun my story and I feel a wave of panic start to overtake me; it's a sick feeling in the pit of my stomach, a pressure in my chest and a fear in my heart. Maybe it's too soon. I take a deep breath and begin to talk gently to myself. I remind myself that these attacks are relatively rare. They happen only a couple of times a year now. Breathe I tell myself. You can get through this, this is nothing compared to what it used to be like. Breathe again, slowly and deeply; think of the positive things in your life. To help cope, I close my eyes and imagine a mother softly humming as she rubs the back of a small child. I have done this before and have learned that practicing positive imagery is an important tool in providing comfort. I smile as this starts to work.

I look down the road I've traveled, back to the beginning, and I take a breath. It wasn't an easy journey, but I was fortunate to have some very wonderful people reach out and touch my life. And while I didn't necessarily realize it at the time the skills and values that they imparted helped me get to where I am today. I finally feel like I deserve all that I have and all that I have accomplished. For years I felt that I had cheated fate; I should have ended up just like my mother, and probably could have. However with hard work and the help of many people, I have left those feelings in the past. Now I have a big smile on my face, I love life, I like myself and I feel I am entitled to all that I have worked so hard to accomplish.

THE EARLY YEARS
2 to 8 years of age

My mother Wanda was born and raised in St. John, New Brunswick, the oldest of six children. She never talked much about her mother, but from the pieces of information she let slip in conversation it was clear that the conflict between them started early and escalated until Wanda left home for good. The problem, everyone kept telling Wanda, was that she was too wild.

As I grew older, I realized that 'wild' really meant she was 'one of the guys' – and in St. John that meant a whole lot of drinking; disappearing for days at a time on a bender. My mother started this behaviour young, and clearly did a lot of damage to herself and those around her. After I became a mother, I took my own children to visit an uncle and my grandparents. My grandfather recognized me and gave me a big hug, my grandmother wouldn't speak to me, claiming that since no one had introduced us, she didn't know who I was.

On that visit to Eastern Canada I felt like I had been thrown back in time; it seemed that women were expected to work, clean and raise the children, while the men went to work and partied with their friends.

Maybe that's why Wanda married an American soldier in 1958 at the age of 17; she wanted to escape her family, her mother and her future in St. John. The marriage only lasted a few years and this would become another pattern in my mother's life. During this brief marriage she moved to the United States and had a little boy, Earl, and a little girl, Mary. This marriage broke down before Mary was two. After the separation Wanda returned to Canada, arriving in Kingston, Ontario.

The two children stayed with their father who later remarried. Visitation with these two children was sporadic, and served mainly to aggravate the new family situation. Wanda said she couldn't keep the children with her unless she returned to her family in St. John, New Brunswick and apparently, that wasn't an option. When she passed away in 1997 at the age of 56, I found the following letter from her mother tucked away in her belongings. Waymon was her father's name.

Wanda

Waymon said faiToot to come down here to live no body wants you, as you would have everyone in trouble, and you would be glad to go back up there, he like me wouldn't let you act like we know you do up there, so you better stay up there where you know everyone.
So don't plan on us,
mom

It was another pattern I would learn to recognize in my mother; if she wasn't happy, then she made sure that no one around her was happy either.

In 1965, Wanda produced yet another child, a girl, and that was me. Wanda's priorities were still having fun and drinking with her friends. Having a child made this a little difficult at times, but she soon had a list of people who would take me in for extended periods of time.

One of these people was Daniel, who I believe loved Wanda for many years and would have been happy to marry her and help raise me. Unfortunately, Wanda was only interested in the second part of that arrangement - Daniel raising her child.

Daniel was a tall, thin man who worked nights driving a tractor trailer. He was gentle and good natured and always had time for my mother and me. He often cared for me when I was an infant and in between relationships for many years, my mother would use Daniel as a caregiver. Looking back, he was definitely a father figure for me. And a good one, I trusted him implicitly.

But nothing ever lasted long for Wanda – before my first birthday she had a new love in her life and everyone else's life had to be turned upside down so Wanda could be happy. My mother married Karl Jamison before I was a year old.

Karl was jealous of Daniel and insisted my mother cut off all contact with him. My mother's first concern was always the latest man in her life, so it didn't matter how much Daniel or I cried. I don't remember a single time when she put any of her children before or even a close second to her latest man.

I only have vague memories of Karl, but I remember I didn't like him much. At that time, my mother worked and Karl stayed home with me. I was hospitalized on various occasions for malnutrition, sometimes so weak that I wasn't even able to cry. I have some memories of Karl from when I was two. He would be sitting on the couch and call me over ever so nicely; I would run over to see what he wanted and then he would throw me over his knee and spank me. I never knew why, or when it would happen and I soon learned to stay out of any room he was in. As I grew a little older the dog and I would stay outside as much as possible. Sometimes at the end of a work day I would meet my mother at the bus stop and walk home with her.

Their relationship didn't last long, if it had ever been more than a drinking relationship. They fought continually in their drunken state. Karl often beat my mother up and the fighting would continue into the early hours of the next day.

During one of these fights, when I was about three and half, a raging Karl threatened my mother with a beer bottle, and my mother told me to get behind the couch. Karl threw the bottle – I don't know who he was aiming at. I didn't feel a thing, but my mother looked at me and began screaming. I could feel something running down my cheek, like beer, or maybe tears, but when I wiped my face with my hand it was covered in blood. That's when I started screaming as well – nothing scared me more than the sight of blood.

I was still screaming when they got me to the hospital. Karl and my mother continued their fight in the waiting room, while I was taken, terrified, to the operating room. When the doctors placed a green cloth over my face, I swore at them and told them my mother would kill them if they didn't get off me. I was terrified of these strangers who were shining bright lights in my one uncovered eye. I continued to scream for my mother who was too busy with her own fight to notice. The bottle had just missed my eye and required stitches; they had to tie me to the table in order to stitch me up and I am sure my mouth never stopped. Even before this incident I was a confused and traumatized child, and this experience didn't make me feel any safer.

When my mother took me to the doctor to have the stitches removed she sat on me on the window sill, while the doctor attempted to remove the stitches from my eye. I was kicking and screaming in pain as he tried plucking out the stitches one at a time. He only managed to get out two or three of the stitches before giving up. The rest of the stitches stayed in until we visited my siblings, Earl and Mary in the United States. When we arrived at the hospital there I was all wound up and started kicking and screaming before they even touched me. When it was over they gave me a sucker and I was surprised to learn that the event was over and I hadn't felt a thing.

Shortly after this event, Wanda and Karl separated, but it had long-lasting effects, some more obvious than others. Hair dressers still wore white coats in those days, and every hair cut triggered my anxiety. My mother would have to sit in the chair and hold me on her lap very tightly so I couldn't get away. However, she couldn't hold my head still and for a few years I had some interesting looking haircuts.

For a brief period, my mom and I lived alone on Montreal Street. She had her friends and her parties, but I don't recall any particular man. However, even when there was no man in her life, my mother was distant and disinterested in me and I was often lonely. I remember finding a dead squirrel in the road and bringing it home so my mother could save it. I was sobbing that the squirrel needed to go to the doctor, as he was very sick. My mother wasn't impressed; she told me to throw him away outside. I went outside, but sat on the front step, dead squirrel in my arms and cried. Some teenage kids from the neighbourhood came along and asked what was wrong. I showed them my squirrel and said it was very sick; they took it and threw it over the train tracks.

Wanda had various mood swings, but they were worse when she was drinking. Sometimes she loved me, sometimes she hated me. Occasionally she felt sorry for me, but mostly she felt sorry for herself; at those times everything was my fault. I could never do or say the right thing, never behave the right way to make her happy. She told me that all her friends used to say, "Here's Wanda and that goddamn kid".

After Karl and my mother split, Daniel was back in the picture and happy to assume his former role as my primary caregiver. Daniel would finish a night shift and go home to sleep. However, my mother would show up shortly after he arrived home to drop me off for the day. I remember how lonely I used to feel trying to find something to do while Daniel slept. Usually, when Daniel woke up he would cook dinner for the two of us and play some games with me before returning me to my mother, and heading back to work.

One night Daniel was over at our house looking after me while my mother was out with her friends. Daniel was lying on the couch watching TV and I was lying on the floor in front of the couch. I had picked up a pack of matches from the base of the coffee table and while I was holding them I thought about lighting one. I figured that since I couldn't really see Daniel he likely couldn't see me either.

I lit the match, absolutely sure that Daniel couldn't see it, but the minute the match burst into flames Daniel's hand came down and snatched the matches, including the lit one from my hands. I was totally surprised that he was so smart and thought I shouldn't try that again.

Daniel's mother lived in Cornwall, and I loved to visit her. I don't remember a lot about her, but I do remember her making me tea with honey as a bedtime snack, along with toast and peanut butter and a bowl of maple syrup to dip it in. I have pictures of me in new pyjamas with some toys at Christmas time. She was very kind to me, but I think that I loved to go there because it was always calm. No one was fighting or drinking and for a few hours I got to feel special. I imagined this was how kids felt when they hung out with their grandparents.

Wanda's apartment was a party place. My mother was usually drunk and all her friends were drunk with her. By the time I was four years old, I spent a lot of time on my own or out on the streets. I was very proud of my ability to wander for blocks, and find my way home. And when I didn't find my way home, my mother would phone the police and get them to look for me. I really enjoyed riding in the police car and chatting with whichever police officer was giving me a ride home this time. It got so the police knew me by name and would pick me up and return me home even before my mother called.

At about this time, my mother's mood swings became more extreme and more unpredictable. I remember once getting permission to watch TV with a little girl next door. It would be dark when the show was over, but her older brother agreed to walk me home. When the show was over, the older brother walked me home as promised, but my mother had already forgotten the agreement. She started screaming at me for not being home before dark. Then she decided that she would punish me for not arriving on time by paddling my behind with her peter meter. A peter meter is a piece of wood with measurement markings on it, used to measure the length of a man's peter. She made me strip down to nothing and then stand in front of her, and not move. As she hit me I couldn't help moving, so she sat on me and continued to hit me with the thick wooden paddle.

I remember this incident in particular, because of the moment of joy I had the following day. Wanda was repeating the story of my beating to her drinking buddies when one of the men who hung around took the peter meter and broke it so she couldn't hit me with it again.

These experiences continued. I don't remember my mother ever being sober during these years; she drank from the time she got up, until the time she passed out.

My mother met Albert when I was four and he quickly became a regular visitor. He was a carpenter by trade, usually working seasonally during the warm weather. I remember him asking me if I would I call him Dad, when he married my mother. This was a strange word to me, as I had never at any time called anyone Dad, and I told Albert I wouldn't use it for him. In fact if any one deserved to be called "Dad" it would have been Daniel.

Albert never married my mother, but they did become a couple. It didn't take Albert long to begin sexually abusing me. My mother was either not home, drunk, or passed out most of the time. When I began to have more tantrums and screaming fits she chose to believe that it was because I was a bad kid. She never acknowledged that there might have been something going on that would cause my bad behaviour.

My mother and Albert decided to move out west in the summer of 1969, so off we went. While we were there the sexual abuse continued. We were staying with a family with a little boy about the same age as myself. I told him about the abuse and of course he told his mother. She felt it necessary to tell my mother. My mother got very angry and called me a liar. At first, she just sent me to bed with no supper. But after sitting and drinking for awhile her anger grew. She decided to punish me. She came and got me out of bed, stripped me and held me up in front of four adults so they could all look between my legs and see that I didn't have any red marks. That proved, she said, that I was lying.

Even at that young age, about four, I was totally and completely humiliated. I knew that I would never speak of what was going on ever again. Albert, of course, used my humiliation to his advantage. Now he had total control and my mother had given it to him. He could get away with anything knowing I wouldn't say a word to anyone. Upon returning to Kingston I had screaming fits every time my mother tried to go out and leave me alone with Albert. This of course only made her angrier. It proved to her that I was just a very bad kid. She made it clear I was only tolerated because she received a welfare cheque for looking after me.

Albert would threaten me with being sent away if I told anyone what was going on, and he didn't have to work very hard to convince me that he was probably telling the truth. It was already clear to me that my mother didn't even like me and wouldn't fight to keep me.

In the fall of 1970, I started kindergarten. I didn't have a problem walking to school, but when I came out of school at noon I would get disoriented and didn't know how to get home. Therefore, the routine was, I got myself up and ready for school and walked there in the morning, and my mother would pick me up at noon after she woke up.

The first day of school was so cool; there were other kids to play with and totally awesome toys, like blocks, books, and paints. I painted a picture for my mom. I was very proud of it and hoped it would make her happy. When my mother arrived to pick me up, I asked the teacher for my picture so I could give it to my mom. The teacher said no because she was hanging it on the wall. I wanted so badly to make my mom happy, and I was so sure this wonderful picture would do just that. When the teacher said that I really couldn't give it to my mom, I had a major temper tantrum, yelling, screaming, cursing and throwing myself around on the floor, shocking both the teacher and my mother. My mother had to drag me out of the classroom and to the car. All she said was, "You're going to get it when you get home". Instead of making her happy, the picture had made her even angrier at me.

However, when we got home she appeared to forget all about the incident. Of course, she hadn't. The punishment came later, when I no longer expected it. This became a pattern. I never knew when I was going to be punished or for what I was being punished. It could be on the same day I was 'bad', or it could be weeks later. Once she had decided to punish me for something she would do it over and over again. I could be punished for weeks or years over a particular event. It is difficult to live in a situation when you never know what the punishment will be, or what it will be for.

It only took a few weeks of school before my mother began to sleep in past noon and not show up at school to get me. I remember standing in the schoolyard crying because I didn't know how to get home. Eventually the crossing guard found me as he walked by the school and pointed me in the right direction.

Once I had mastered the skill of getting to and from school on my own, I noticed that the boy upstairs rode his bike to school and I started to ask for a bike. On his birthday in the fall of that year he received a new bike, so I asked if I could ride his old bike to school. He wouldn't let me ride it, so when he wasn't looking I took it and rode it to school anyway. After school I decided to leave the bike at school and walk home. My mother met me half-way home and asked where the bike was. I insisted I had no clue what she was talking about, but back to school we marched. My mother was not convinced by my surprise at finding the neighbour's bike right there in the bike rack. She was furious and surprisingly quiet as we hustled home to return the bike. Once the bike was returned and I had apologized to the neighbour, my mother went into the house and retrieved her matches. In the driveway, in front of everyone, she lit a couple of matches and held my hand over the flame. This, she said, is what happens to thieves. None of the people watching this intervened.

I adjusted to my mother's schedule at an early age – sleep until sometime in the afternoon and be up all night. Getting up for school was sometimes hard to do, as my mother often kept me up until four or five in the morning when she would finally pass out. If I missed school, she would be very angry with me. She seemed to be unaware that we hadn't gone to bed until 5 a.m.

I remember pleading with her friends not to leave, not to leave me alone with her. She could be happy one moment, and then she would become extremely nasty. When she was alone, I wasn't allowed to go to bed. My job was to keep her company until she passed out. I was expected to look after her, but she would usually be angry at me for things that had happened a long time ago or which I had no control over. Once she was angry because when we were at someone's house I was given something to eat along with the other children, and I hadn't saved her some. I paid attention and I learned quickly; if someone fed me when we were out I made sure to save half for my mother. But I also learned that it didn't matter, she would just be angry about something else instead. I was living in a perpetual 'no win' situation.

Although I had good reason to throw tantrums, I knew better than to do more than breathe when she was drinking heavily. If I could keep out of her way, I did. During the day it was pretty easy to stay out of the way, but the night was a whole different story. I know that lots of kids are afraid of the dark, but I was terrified of the dark. Not because of unseen monsters, but because I knew what was going to happen. There was no escape, and everyone or anyone who might intervene would be sleeping and unavailable. The worst things always happened at night: the fighting, the beatings, the sexual abuse and the terror. In daylight you could dream that today would be the day someone was going to save you, even knowing how unlikely that really was. But in the dark I couldn't even cling to that dream. All I could do was close my eyes and pray for the darkness to end.

By the time I was six my mother's rages were terrible – she would yell, scream and hit me. I had learned to stop crying, because tears just made her angrier, but now it seemed that my not crying made her angry too. More and more often, she threatened to get rid of me. She said I was more trouble than I was worth. I still didn't cry but these statements increased my stress as they proved that Albert was right; my mother wasn't ever going to listen to me or save me from him. I needed someone to save me from both of them.

I was only about six the first time she threw me out of the house. It was February, very cold, and I couldn't believe she meant it. It was dark. Where would I go? I didn't know what to do or how to calm her down. I tried agreeing with her and promising to do better. I agreed it was all my fault and I was very sorry. Nothing worked!

I had to use the washroom before I left. I was so scared that I thought I might pee my pants. She yelled and screamed, while I was on the toilet and then pulled me off to throw me out of her house. She refused to let me take my boots or coat, as she had bought these items and they were hers.

So there I was freezing on Rideau Street standing in the snow in leotards and a dress, not knowing what to do or where to go. Other children were outside playing, but I didn't know what to do. I sat on the front step of the house crying.

Daniel showed up and took me back into the house. He said my mother had called him and told him she had kicked me out and didn't know where I was. That was the first of many similar experiences, but it was the one and only time my mother ever apologized to me.

My mother and Albert continued to drink and fight. One day I came home from school for lunch and my mother had no front teeth. When I asked her what had happened she said she had gone to the dentist and had them pulled out. As she was still in her housecoat, and was never normally even up at this time, I was pretty sure Albert had punched her in the mouth and knocked her teeth out.

When they both drank, which was most of the time, the fights would be continuous. My mother would scream for me and it was my job to protect her. I learned quickly after the first fight when I did nothing but hide that this was not the appropriate response. I was supposed to phone the police.

During her marathon drinking bouts, I was not allowed to eat 'her' food; sometimes I went three and four days with nothing to eat. I remember one day waking up and feeling so dizzy and tired, I barely made it down stairs. I put two pieces of bread in the toaster, but fell asleep at the kitchen table before they popped. When I woke up I ate the cold and dry toast, glad that I hadn't been caught eating.

I wasn't always so lucky. On another occasion, I snuck a piece of pizza from the box under my mother's bed. I took a bite, then thought better of it and put the piece back. When my mother discovered the pizza with a bite taken out of it, she threw me across the room. I landed on the electric heater hard enough to smash it into pieces.

When my mother wasn't abusing me, she expected me to look after her. During these long drinking binges, it wasn't unusual for her to have an asthma attack, and it was always my responsibility to look out for her and call the ambulance. Once, I remember the fire department showing up. They opened the windows and provided care for my mother. My mother never said thank you. She just expected me to provide her with the care that she never gave me.

When we lived on Bay Street we shared a driveway with our neighbour Shelly. Although I was terrified of the big Doberman that Shelly kept tied in the driveway, I was grateful for Shelly's kindness towards me. She even bought me a new bike with her tax refund one year. After we moved from Bay Street, Shelly would take me in when my mother kicked me out at two or three in the morning. Sometimes I would have to walk 10-12 blocks in the middle of the night to get to Shelly's house and no sooner would I arrive than my mother would call Shelly and demand she send me back home. Shelly would tell her to sleep it off and I would come home tomorrow. I think Shelly tried reporting my mother to Children's Aid a few times, but it didn't seem to help.

I would arrive home after school the next day and my mother would act like nothing had happened – although she insisted Shelly had bed bugs and that was why I had red spots all over me. I was never uncomfortable when I stayed with Shelly, she would watch TV with me, make me something to eat and talk with me about school. While I didn't believe that Shelly had bed bugs, I was often tempted to tell my mother that given a choice, I would happily take the bed bugs over her, any day.

I was very grateful that during this time in my life Shelly was always there when I needed somewhere to sleep for the night and she was always happy to feed me. I have no idea how I could have got through that time in my life without her.

After Albert moved in with us, Daniel stopped expecting my mother to return the love he had once felt for her, or maybe she destroyed that love. He moved on, found a wonderful woman to love, and married her. Even though she had rejected him, my mother did her best to destroy his marital relationship; she didn't want Daniel as her boyfriend or anything like that, but she liked having him at her beck and call. She would often call him in the middle of the night, needing something and he often showed up to help. Time passed and soon I only saw Daniel once or twice a year, but every time it was like we had never been apart. I missed Daniel very much and it was clear that he missed me just as much and this seemed to be another reason for jealousy. When I was little I couldn't say 'Daniel', so I had always called him Bobby and I continued to call him Bobby, even after I could say his name. However, after one of his rare visits, when Daniel left, Albert became very angry at me for calling him Bobby and I was told never to call Daniel that again. I never did, and the loss of my special name for him seemed to widen the gap between Daniel and myself.

Albert abused me from the time I was four until I left my mother's house, five years later. I hated going to see his family in Odessa. I often threw screaming fits when we had to go for the weekend. Going to his family's meant being surrounded with people who were drinking and fighting all day and night, and there was nowhere to go because they lived in the country. During one of our weekend visits we were all sleeping in the same bed. Albert was in the middle as my mother refused to sleep in the middle. As we all lay there in bed, Albert had his hands all over me and I was moving around trying to get as far away from him as possible. My mother's reaction? She just got angry that I was keeping her awake and yelled at me to lay still.

Sometimes it is really hard to believe she didn't know. Sometimes I think that she did know, but it was fine if it meant Albert wasn't going to leave her.

I recall coming home from school one day to find my mother on the couch and her lips all green – she had decided to take all her 'nerve' pills. I was terrified that she might be dead, and called the ambulance again. When the police and Albert showed up, the officer told me I could stay with my mother or go with Albert. I do remember thinking, 'Wow, what a choice - the dead woman or the sexual predator'. In the end, the thought of staying with my dead mother was worse than going with the sexual predator. At least I knew what to expect. I was terrified of my mother, dead or alive.

My life was like being trapped in a big nightmare, and no matter which way I turned there were monsters. One evening around dinner time I went to the store for my mother, it was only a couple of blocks away. About a block from my home, a friendly man approached me and offered to carry my bag for me. We walked along talking and when I said goodbye and turned to take my bag back from him, he was standing there fully exposed from his waist to his knees. I started screaming and ran into the house. Of course, by the time anyone came to look he was long gone. I was sure that he was going to come back and climb into my bedroom window and this gave me even more nightmares. At this point in my life I was learning that no man, however friendly he seemed, should ever be trusted. With the exception of Daniel who was practically in the past now, all men were the same; they preyed on children, especially young girls, relentlessly.

My mother, Albert and I shared the bedroom in our one bedroom apartment on Bay street. The room was always a mess and eventually my mother decided this was my fault as well. She ordered me to clean-up the bedroom. I wasn't quite sure what she wanted me to do, as I hadn't cleaned anything before, so I began to empty the ashtrays. While I was picking up the ashtrays I noticed that my mother's bed had a hole in the side of the mattress, where the handle had been pulled out. So instead of emptying the ashtrays, I sat beside the bed lighting matches and throwing them in the hole. I hated that room and I hated the memories associated with it. I had often been chased from bed to bed by Albert. I hated Albert for that, hated my mother for having allowed or ignored it, and I especially hated that bed. I felt very desperate and perhaps I thought that if there was no bed, the problem would be solved. After throwing a dozen matches in the hole I left the bedroom, closed the door and told my mother I was going outside to play. One of the matches must have stayed lit, because shortly afterwards I watched the fire department arrive and put out the burning mattress.

My mother knew who had set the bed on fire, but I was never punished. She never mentioned it; not even when she was in a drunken fit and remembering everything else 'bad' I had ever done. This added credibility to my belief that she was fully aware of what Albert was up to.

Wally was a friendly young man who lived across the street from our Bay street apartment. He would build snow forts with me, bring me Twinkies from his delivery truck, and let me sit on his knee in the car and pretend to drive. He told me how much he loved me, how he would wait for me to grow up so he could marry me. He seemed to love me, and I loved him very much for that. Which of course made it easy for him to sexually abuse me. I liked to spend time with him so much I didn't mind the other stuff. He never hurt me and was always so nice to me. Besides, I was learning that this was natural behaviour, so better to have someone who you liked take advantage of you than someone you didn't like. I didn't have anyone else who even pretended to care about me. I was furious when he announced he was getting married. I felt betrayed and I couldn't even talk to him. Now there was no one who wanted me, and no hope that someday he would save me from this life. Having your dreams destroyed is a wound that only leaves marks on the inside.

After he got married he told me he felt bad and invited me to visit while his wife was at work so he could show me how sorry he was. I refused but his younger brother Don wanted to take over where Wally left off. I never liked Don and did my best to avoid him; however, his father and my mother were drinking buddies so sometimes I couldn't always dodge him. A couple of years after his marriage, Wally's mother died, and he committed suicide shortly after this. Everyone believed it was because of his mother's death, but I knew he had other secrets. His taking advantage of me had told me that much.

Wanda and Albert fought continuously over nothing and everything it seemed. They fought over who drank the last beer, who was sleeping with who. In fact, I think my mother being in her drunken stupor most of the time, may have made it through all of Albert's 14 brothers. Eventually I learned to see these fights coming and to get out of the way. The worst fights seemed to occur only when both parties were drinking. If Albert drank and my mother didn't there was no fight, but when they both drank, my mother wouldn't let anything go, she just wouldn't stop arguing for anything. The first stage was a period of yelling and screaming at each other. Then Albert would start telling her to shut her bleeping mouth, which just made my mother rant more; she wouldn't stop for anything now. Next came the physical threats and then Albert would be beating the shit out of my mother, and she would be screaming, "Brenda! Help me! Call the police! Get him off me, he is going to kill me, Brenda!"

I'd go for the phone but Albert would pull out the phone cords, so then I would run to the neighbours, sobbing, asking them to call the police because my mom's boyfriend was hurting her very badly. Then I would run back to the front of the house and listen to the fight, as I waited for the police to arrive. After that happened a few times, Albert started beating my mother up in the doorway of the room we were in, so I couldn't get out to call police – then I would crawl out the window. No one ever seemed to notice that the police needed to be called, until I showed up at their door. They would always call the police for me, and some tried to invite me in to wait for the police, but I never went in. I knew that if I did my mother would be very angry at me. I was supposed to be saving her, not having someone feel sorry for me. After they assured me they would call the police immediately, I would return to listen to my mother scream, and wait.

The police always arrived fairly quickly, and they always did the same thing. They asked Albert to leave the house for the evening and he, of course, was very polite to the officers. He always explained that if my mother could just shut her mouth we wouldn't be having this problem. The officers always seemed very understanding of Albert and waited for him to clean himself up. Then they could give him a ride to wherever he was going to spend the night. For my mother the worst was over, but the nightmare was just beginning for me.

I feared many things as a kid, but my greatest fear was being alone with my drunken mother at 3 a.m. after she had a big fight with Albert. She could stay up for hours, often not falling asleep before 7 or 8 o'clock in the morning. She would go through many emotional states in a single night. First, she would feel sorry for me and for not being a good mother and looking after me. Then she would feel sorry for herself, what she had missed in life, and the rotten brat of a kid she got stuck with. She would get angry with me, and would remember everything I had ever done to upset her. It didn't matter if these things had happened years ago, she would remember every incident and get angrier and angrier. I tried apologizing, I agreed with her on everything, I promised to try harder, to do a better job. But it didn't matter what was said. When Wanda worked herself up into this sort of frenzy nothing could be said to console her. There was no way of avoiding her wrath.

After she had told me all the ways I had ruined her life, the real viciousness would begin. She would tell me she knew who my father was but she would make sure I never found out. She told me that she would occasionally call him but he didn't want anything to do with me even when she told him that Children's Aid might come and get me. His answer? "Not my problem." She reminded me that although she had put Earl and Mary's father's name on my birth certificate that was only because they were still legally married. I would never find out who my father was.

As her anger grew I would get more scared, because I knew that it wouldn't stop at words. I always tried not to set her off, but I never knew what the final straw would be. Sometimes just using her washroom without asking was all it took, or even just leaving the room. I remember once running to her bathroom, so scared I thought I would pee my pants. I had just sat down on the toilet and she flew into the bathroom and yanked me off the toilet kicking and pushing me out of the washroom. I scrambled to drag up my pants, trying to stand up and get out of the way, as she was swinging and kicking and pushing me out of the way. I was terrified that she would throw me out onto the street before I could get my pants pulled up. I often ended up in the middle of the street at 4 or 5 in the morning, crying, as she screamed at me to get out of her house and never come back. I wished I could never come back too.

Wanda didn't always become physically violent during these all-night benders. Sometimes it involved psychological abuse – that I didn't deserve to eat her food, I wasn't worth the cost of the groceries so I could just leave her food alone. I would spend many hours making her happy, getting her a roll of toilet paper, making her something to eat, getting her another drink, but nothing I did was ever right. She would pass out in the early morning, and I would fall asleep right after she did. If I tried to sleep while she was awake this would anger her too, so I always stayed awake until she fell asleep. When she awoke later in the day, if I was still sleeping, I would be in trouble for missing school. It didn't matter that I wasn't allowed to go to bed until after she did, and many times I had to stand at the foot of her bed, while she fell asleep, reminding me of what a burden I was. Sometimes when she seemed to be sleeping, and I would try to sneak off to bed only to hear her yelling out for me. It was easier to stand there an extra-long time, than to run the risk that she might get back up and continue yelling at me. With time, I learned to wake up about a half hour before she did, leave the house and come home at lunchtime or the end of the day, pretending I had been at school. Wanda would wake up, grab a drink and continue on where she had left off. This could go on for three or more days, and every night I hoped she would kick me out. Once she kicked me out, it seemed we got to start fresh all over again. Perhaps she felt bad about kicking a small child out in the middle of the night.

My first suicide attempt was at the age of 7. Since setting the bed on fire hadn't worked, I had a new plan. I remember the incident, but only recently have I remembered the feelings that went with it. I walked home from school every day, down a big hill on Ordnance Street and across a busy street that ran through the middle of the hill. While walking home I remember thinking, I would do anything not to have to go home and encounter my mother and her drunken friends. The turmoil in that house caused me a great deal of anxiety and fear. I never knew what to expect or who to fear on any given day. I decided during my walk that if I were to run down the hill and into the street I would be hit by a car and perhaps I would never have to go home again. So when I reached the halfway point on the hill I began to run as fast I could down the hill, picking up speed along the way. Then around the corner and out between two parked cars and into the middle of the road.

It turns out that this wasn't such a great plan. I had mistimed it. Instead of running into the car head-on, I had only grazed the side of the car and was thrown backwards. The frightened driver wanted to take me home. Oops that one backfired! I told the driver I was OK, and ran home on my own. Later that night the driver showed up at the door to see if I was actually OK. She had watched what street I turned on and then went door to door along the street to find me. My botched suicide attempt only ended up leaving me with some bruises, put me back on my mother's black list (as if I ever got off it), and scared the hell out of a stranger. It left me wondering, "what else could a 'bad' kid do to make an exit from this terrible world".

Many times as a small child, I would eat all the pills I could find in the house and in my mother's purse. There were several trips to emergency and then my mother would have to keep me from sleeping to make sure I was fine. In her own sarcastic way she let me know how much she really enjoyed that job.

When I was eight my mother had her fourth child, a little girl who weighed about three pounds when she was born. My mother was drunk for her entire pregnancy and we would later see the results of that in my little sister.

When my little sister cried in the middle of the night, my mother would scream at me to heat a bottle for her. Of course, I never did it fast enough for her. So while I waited for the bottle warmer to do its job, I had to listen to both my sister and my mother screaming.

At this point there was plenty of violence in my life. My mother and Albert fought and beat on each other regularly. My mother and I fought continually. And, it was my full time job to try and avoid situations where I was left home alone with Albert. I was attending Rideau Heights Public School and my 'accidents' became more and more common. One day, riding my bike back to school I began turning my handle bars back and forth as far as I could in either direction while peddling downhill as fast as I could go. Sure enough I took a header, but once again I was disappointed. It wasn't fatal, and my mother was angry about having to come to school to collect me with my most recent injuries.

In spite of my numerous suicide attempts I was still left with inescapable responsibilities at home. One day at school the secretary came to get me and told me that my mother had called and would like me to come home early. I was excited and skipped all the way home as I was sure she was going to take me skating, something she had been promising to do for some time now. When I arrived home I found the real reason for taking me out of school early – my mother needed me to look after my sister, while she slept off the alcohol. Wanda often left me to babysit my sister while she went out drinking. I liked my little sister, but I didn't like having to spend all my time looking after her.

One night shortly after Wanda had left for a night of drinking, the building superintendent showed up looking for my mother. I said she wasn't home. The super said she was calling the Children's Aid Society (CAS). This scared me, not because I was afraid of the CAS, but because I knew my mother would be angry. So I gathered up my baby sister, her bottle, and headed upstairs to a friend of my mother's. The idea being to stay with my mother's friend until my mother returned. But that didn't work; the CAS showed up at her door and took us both into their care for a short time.

FORM 11
The Child Welfare Act

ORDER

Under Subsection 8 of Section 25 of the Act

In the   Provincial Court (Family Division), County of Frontenac
                  (name of court)

Before   The Presiding Judge   Thurs day, the   20th
             (name of judge)
                              day of   June   , 19 74

In the matter of   Lee Secor
                       (name of child)

a child apparently in need of protection.

Child of   Mrs. Wanda Alice Jamieson
                    (name of parent)

And in the matter of an application by the Children's Aid Society of the City of Kingston and County
                          (name of society)   of Frontenac

I order, the hearing of this matter having been adjourned to the   4th   day of   July   ,

1974   , at 86 Clarence Street, 2nd Floor   at 1:30 o'clock in the after noon,
               (name of place)

that the child be detained in the temporary care and custody of the Children's Aid Society of the City of Kingston and County of Frontenac, 173 Princess Street, Kingston

         (name)   (address)
                                 during the period of adjournment

Statement of the facts upon which this decision is based:

On June 18, 1974, while on emergency duty, I received a telephone call that the two children had been left alone and the mother was said to be intoxicated. No adequate babysitting arrangements had been made and the mother did not appear capable of looking after the children.

                                       (signature of judge)

20-00-011 (6/72)

38

FOSTER CARE
8 to 14 years of age

My introduction to foster care came in June '73. My sister and I found ourselves placed in a foster home after the police came to our apartment and found us home alone. I was eight; my baby sister was six months of age. I had been left to babysit while my mother was out drinking at the local bar.

The Grippen's had three children: a 19-year-old son, a 15-year-old son, and an adopted daughter who was 8 - the same age as me. They lived in the country and seemed like a nice family at first. However, even before I realized that the Grippen's had separate cupboards for food for the foster children, I realized there were issues here as well. Any child in a normal family would not have faced what me and my sister faced. Allow me to explain.

I was put to bed most nights right after supper, because I didn't eat all of my supper. I yelled and screamed and swore on the second or third night and had a half bottle of dish soap poured down my throat for that offence.

The little girl and I fought a lot, and it always ended the same way. She would tattle on me and, I would deny everything. My foster mother's treatment for swearing was soap, but her treatment for lying was Tabasco sauce. Every time she would begin with me, and I would say I wasn't lying. Then I had to swallow a tablespoon of the Tabasco sauce, no drink allow. It felt like I couldn't breathe as tears ran from my eyes. She would ask me again if I was lying and I would shake my head no, and be forced to have another tablespoon of Tabasco sauce. In the end it didn't matter who had done what, the daughter never had to taste the Tabasco sauce. If the daughter misbehaved and I said I was going to tell on her, I had to go to bed for blackmailing the daughter.

Then the oldest son showed me a game he and his sister played. He took off my clothes, then his sister's and laid us on his bed in the basement. He rubbed himself naked on one of us, and then moved over to the other, back and forth. Finally he would ejaculate on our stomachs.

After a couple of weeks of trying to adjust to the Grippen's, my mother's place began to look pretty good. I used the phone in the basement to call my mother, crying and saying I wanted to come home. I got caught on the phone, and was immediately punished with a wooden spoon on my hands. When the punishment was over my hands and finger joints were swollen and bruised. When their own children got into trouble they were beaten with a wooden spoon on the bottom of their feet, I am guessing this is so that it didn't show, but it might have been that it was more painful as they would need to walk on their feet on a continual basis.

When the social worker came for her one visit with me and asked if I liked the Grippen's, I said I did because I was afraid if I complained she would tell them, making things even more difficult than they already were.

Anyway, after a month and a day with the Grippen's, we were returned home to my mother and Albert. My mother was mad at me because she felt it was my fault that my sister and I were taken away by the CAS. I guess going out drinking and leaving two small children home alone had nothing to do with it. Life continued with the same pattern as before. The intervention by the CAS had no effect on my mother's behaviour.

One night after we got back, my mother answered the door and three people came into the apartment. Two of them started to hit my mother with a baseball bat while the third one guarded the door. One of the people was angry about something my mother had said or done. My mother eventually locked herself in the bathroom while I was hiding in the bottom of the closet. One of the intruders found me in the closet and told me it was OK, they were just upset with my mother.

Shortly after returning home we moved to a townhouse on York Street and I began to attend Frontenac Public School. I also began telephoning CAS on a regular basis; their response was that they would get me a Big Sister to take me out to lunch. I began to keep my favourite possessions packed in a special red backpack that my grandmother had sent me as a birthday gift. I kept this bag at school, so I would be ready when Children's Aid finally came to get me. As time passed, I realized no one was coming to rescue me, so I took my bag back home. Incidents were getting worse at home. I was missing a lot of school and was often very hungry. I tried to stay out of the way, but I was constantly needed to care for my sister. I had very few friends, as it is hard to play and push a stroller at the same time. I had become my sister's primary care giver since no one else seemed to care what she was doing, as long as she wasn't crying.

I remember a trip to the broken down bus we used as a cottage, with Albert driving (and drinking), my mother in the passenger seat and me in the middle. I was old enough to know he shouldn't be drinking and told my mother so, but they were having a heated discussion and both helping themselves to the bottle of liquor in my lap. I decided if I drank the liquor Albert wouldn't have any more to drink, so while they argued I finished off the bottle of liquor, much to Albert's dismay. Despite my attempts to keep him sober, Albert put the car in the ditch and then hollered at my mother for drinking all the liquor.

My mother and I set out with a flashlight to find help to tow the car from the ditch, but I was hoofing it far ahead of her. I wasn't waiting, I had told her not to let him drive, but no one ever listened to me. When we got to the bus that we used as a cottage, I went to bed, while my mother went to find help for the car and the drunk in the ditch. Initially I was afraid to be all alone in the dark. But it wasn't long before the liquor put me to sleep.

My mother liked to drink with friends, but the friends never lasted long. For a while she was friendly with the Whalen's who had three children all around the same age as me. Wanda and I stayed for a sleepover one night; the men were out drinking, the women and children were at home. When bedtime arrived, sleeping arrangements were made – the Whalen children shared one room, Mrs. Whalen in her room, Wanda in the other child's room, and me on the couch downstairs, alone. Sometime during the night the men came home, drunk. I was woken up by Mr. Whalen tugging on my clothes, and trying to put his hands under my clothes. I was instantly wide-awake, fearful, knowing exactly what his intentions were. I whispered that I needed to go to the bathroom, and got up and quietly climbed the stairs to the bathroom. Once upstairs, I began peeking in rooms to find my mother; I knew no one would try to come and get me out of bed with her. Unfortunately, I woke Mrs. Whalen (if she wasn't already awake), who started yelling at me for sneaking around the house and waking everyone up. She yelled loud enough to wake my mother. Mrs. Whalen was very angry, and I of course couldn't say anything except that I needed to use the washroom. My mother was mad at me as well for causing such a commotion and there was nothing I could do to change that. I knew beyond a doubt what would happen if I told them why I was really upstairs. Mrs. Whalen would be upset with my mother for having a child that could make up such lies, and my mother would be mad at me because Mrs. Whalen was mad at her. I knew her rant by heart. How she had no friends because they could not stand that rotten lying little brat of hers. Everything was my fault and I was more trouble than I was worth, if it wasn't for the cheque she received for having me, she would be rid of me faster than you could blink an eye. And that would just be the immediate reaction. During most future binges, I would be reminded of this, and re-punished – kicked out in the middle of the night, or not allowed to have food for days at a time. So I said nothing, and listened to the ranting until I'm told to get into bed with my mother. I climb onto the edge of the bed and I don't move a muscle, careful not to make her angrier yet.

The incident with Mr. Whalen is something that almost happened. But I wasn't so fortunate another time and remained unclear about what exactly did happen until many years later. I remember waking up one morning, it could have been afternoon but it was the beginning of the day to me, and feeling so sick and dizzy that I could hardly walk to the bathroom. My whole body ached. I sat down on the toilet and noticed that there was this pink sticky stuff, kind of like blood, all over the inside of my thighs. I cleaned it up and went back to bed because I was feeling so ill. I didn't tell anyone. I had learned not to expect help from adults, at the time I had no idea what had happened.

Things finally changed when I showed up at school with my face all bruised. My mother had gotten mad at me for some reason, it could have been any reason or no reason, and she sat on me with my hands and arms pinned and repeatedly punched and slapped me in the face. At school the next day, the guidance counsellor asked me what happen, and as I was sick and tired of protecting her I smiled and said, "Oh, my mother got mad at me and punched me."

After all it is hard to call someone a liar when they are standing in front of you with bruises all over them. If my mother found out that I had complained about her all she could do was hit me some more. That was going to happen anyway. So rather than being afraid to say anything, I decided to tell someone in authority to see if something would change. Somehow I had always known that my life was not 'normal', although I don't think I had an understanding of normal so much as I knew things could be different. They had to be. I was tired of looking after my mother and sister, while being abused by my mother and her companions.

There is no doubt in my mind that this was why the CAS finally showed up at the school with my little sister and rescued me. I was very happy and very scared at the same time. My last foster care experience had not been what I had hoped for. But right now it seemed like anywhere else was better than returning home with my mother.

Here are The Children's Aid Society case notes from this time. This source provides a different perspective, but the bottom line is the same. My sister and I were existing in a living hell.

Workers Case Notes:
Period Summarized: **Nov 29, 1974 to May 1975:**

> *Contacts with family occurred on Nov 29, Dec 7, Feb 27, March 4, and April 2 and May 1.*
>
> *Collateral contact: Brenda Allen, vice-principal of Frontenac Public School and Lynda Longley of Frontenac Public School.*

Focus & Movement: Lori Allen of Frontenac Public School reported to us in November that Brenda Secor had arrived at school with bruises around her eyes stating that her mother had done this while she was drinking. When I talked to Mrs. Jamieson about the bruises she freely admitted having done this to Brenda when the child was disobedient. She also explained that Brenda was forced to spend her evenings in her bedroom alone because she had interrupted a television program by a constant barrage of questions and comments.

Mrs. Jamieson's complaints about Brenda were numerous. She described her as belligerent, insolent, sneaky, deceitful, and greedy. The problems with her seemed to have started when she was about three years of age, i.e. wandering away from home.

46

When she turned five, she often played hookey from school and would have to be marched back to the classroom.

When discussing this family with Lynda Longley, Child Care Worker, it appears that Brenda is a bright and co-operative child in the classroom. Her attendance is good but lately the teacher has noticed that she is more aggressive and bold toward her.

On Feb. 2: *I received a call from a neighbour stating that Mrs. Jamieson was very often drunk and unable to cope with her children. He also said that Albert had beat Wanda up and she had subsequently laid an assault charge against him. This was substantiated by a weekend emergency worker, who went out to visit Wanda after Albert had beaten her up. The emergency worker went out to talk to Wanda and found her drinking with a girl friend but all seemed well and quiet.*

On Feb 28: *a call was received from a neighbour who stated that Albert and Wanda had been fighting over the weekend and Albert had taken the baby to his parents' home. He apparently wanted this neighbour to request information on how he was to obtain custody. The neighbour also stated that she was concerned about Brenda as she has not been to school all week. A few days later I received a call from Mr. Webster, Wanda's lawyer, requesting that we take some action in retrieving the baby from Albert. I explained* *what our position was and that we would not be able to interfere in a custody matter.*

March 14: *police called the weekend worker, stating that Albert had been arrested for harassing Wanda and mother had been taken to hospital. The children were apparently on their own. When the emergency worker arrived the mother had returned from hospital and was in the midst of a choking spell. She had been to hospital for oxygen. The worker felt that Wanda had been drinking but at the same time thought she was capable of caring for the children.*

March 22: *the emergency worker was called at one o'clock in the morning by Policewoman Knight. Wanda had apparently sent Brenda to spend the night with a neighbour. Then later that night Wanda had changed her mind and decided she wanted Brenda to come home. She had been doing a lot of heavy drinking and the neighbour was afraid to return Brenda to her. The police were finally called and Wanda was persuaded to wait until morning.*

April 26: *a neighbour called the weekend worker stating that Brenda had telephoned her at ten o'clock that evening saying that she was frightened by the drinking going on in the house. The worker went to the home and it was full of people, mostly men, all of whom were very drunk. Both children were in bed so she left. Later that evening the same neighbour reported that Brenda had* *arrived at her friend's home at 1:15 am. after having been sent by her mother to retrieve a carpet sweeper. The child was afraid to go home because she said her mother had swallowed 75 nerve pills along with her beer and was sick. This neighbour went to Wanda's house and found her semiconscious and so took the baby to her house where she kept both children until Albert picked them up in the morning. Another neighbour later told me the same story of Brenda being out late at night and Mrs. Jamieson making a suicide attempt with the pills.*

__May 1:__ Brenda called me at my house in the evening, crying that she was afraid to stay at home because her mother was drinking and fighting with her. I arrived at the house around 7:30PM and could hear the shouting before I even had knocked. I found Wanda drunk, Brenda sitting on a chair in the room with her and Albert. The baby was screaming up in her room. I told them I considered these repeated drinking episodes serious enough to take the case to the family Court and that I would return in the morning. I was prepared to remove the children that evening, however I knew there would be a great fuss and I did not feel this would be a healthy experience for either of the children. I went back to the house with another worker and saw Brenda still sitting on the chair in the front room with her mother. Wanda appeared very drunk at this point. I asked Albert to put Brenda and the baby to bed and he did.

Tentative Diagnosis: _Wanda seems to be going downhill during this period. There has been frequent drinking episodes and incident of child abuse, and considerable marital problems between her and Albert. Still Wanda will not admit that she has a drinking problem and states that she drinks only with her friends to have a good time and is never without her senses. When confronted with some of these episodes she usually denies or confuses them or else puts the blame on someone else, usually the person who complained. Brenda is aware that I am concerned about her and as a result in May called me at home. I think that some of her antagonistic behavior in the classroom is due in a great part to the instability in the home the last few months._

It is difficult working with Wanda as she won't admit she has problems and therefore will not accept any help. She continues to blame Brenda for many of her problems and will not look to herself as the cause of some of these. I am sure that in the near future this case will have to be heard in Family Court since there does not seem any other way of getting through to Wanda. Perhaps a supervisory order might make her realize that further authorities will become involved if she doesn't improve.

Casework Plans and Goals: _I am planning at this point to remove both children from the home for a temporary period of time or_ *until a supervisory order can be put into effect. The reasons for doing so are:*

> *(1) To make Wanda realize that she will have to accept some help for her drinking,*
>
> *(2) To realize that she owes it to the children to provide them with a more stable life, and*
>
> *(3) To make Albert improve the situation as much as he can.*

Period Summarized: **May 1, 1975- November 1, 1975**

Frequent contacts were made with both the parents and Brenda. Collateral contacts took place with Mr. Webster, Wanda's lawyer, the father on record in New York and Bud Davids of the Kingston Police Force.

Court Hearings: On **May 29, 1975** *a six month supervisory order was granted on Brenda Secor. The younger child remained in the care of her parents. On July 31, 1975 Brenda Secor was made a temporary ward of our agency for a period of eight months.*

Focus & Movement: On May 7th I obtained a warrant from the court and apprehended both children, after having received several complaints from Brenda mostly regarding the amount of *drinking and fighting going on in the home. On May 29th the baby was returned to her parents under a six month supervisory order. Brenda was made a temporary ward of the Children's Aid Society on July 31, 1975 for a period of eight months. Wanda seemed most upset by this apprehension and court appearance and I feel that it might have shocked the parents into realizing our concerns regarding the care they were giving their children. However, on May the 29th Wanda called the emergency worker and sounded drunk. She asked for visits for Brenda during this period and cried about the loss of her child. As the condition of supervisory order Wanda was ordered to attend the Addiction Unit of the Kingston Psychiatric Hospital. She began this program on June 25th and it was to last for a period of three weeks.*

Phone contact was made with Brenda's natural father who lives in Oswego, New York. He stated that he had not seen Brenda since 1970 and that he indeed was not the natural father, he had six children and did not feel that he could take on a seventh. Therefore he was consenting to the temporary wardship order for Brenda.

<u>On July 21:</u> *Brenda had a visit with her mother and on August 19th Brenda had a weekend visit with her family. On October 6 a police officer from the Kingston Police force, a Mr. Bud Davids came to the agency stating that Wanda was drunk the night before and as he did not feel that she was capable of looking after the* *baby he took the child to a relative's house and asked that this woman care for the baby until morning. He stated that she was drunk 99% of the time and that he had been called out several times to the home to stop fights. He also stated that she had been beaten by Albert at this time. On October 14th I visited Wanda, just after she arrived home with two other men. She had been drinking and appeared very upset and concerned as Albert had apparently beaten her badly that weekend. She complains regularly of Albert's brother being around the house and upsetting her husband. She admitted that she was upset at Albert and in order to calm herself down was drinking again and popping pills. She made a comment that "more liquor goes in and out of this place than in any of the local breweries". She also stated that when Albert gets paid a big drunk occurs. Wanda seemed concerned and now that she is working at Kingston Spinners on three shifts that Albert, rather than caring for the baby himself is placing her with a babysitter. On October 25 the emergency weekend worker was called by the police to state that Wanda was drunk and upset regarding the loss of Brenda and an incident where a man attempted suicide at her place. This did not seem to involve Wanda however.*

PROVINCIAL COURT (FAMILY DIVISION) FOR THE COUNTY OF FRONTENAC

In the Matter of the Child Welfare Act of Ontario

TO: Wanda Alice Jamieson

In the matter of _____ Lee Secor **and** Baby Sister _____

      This is to advise you that the Children's Aid Society for the City of Kingston and the County of Frontenac will be applying to the Judge at the Family Court at 86 Clarence Street, Kingston, Ontario, for a short adjournment of the protection case involving the child(ren) mentioned above. The application will be made on <u>Thursday the 8th</u> day of <u>May</u> next at <u>9:15</u>. The Children's Aid Society will be asking for an Order which would leave the child(ren) in its care until the date of the hearing.

      You may appear to state your wishes regarding these requests to be made by the Children's Aid Society. If you do not appear, and the adjournment is granted, you will be given full notice of the date on which the case will be heard.

DATED this <u>8th</u> day of <u>May</u>, 197<u>5</u>.

Date: _May 9/75_

This Notice was ~~served upon~~ _left at the_

house of Wanda Jamieson

by _E. Willan_

54

My opinion about the preceding case notes is that the system moved very slowly. I am not sure if the worker thought the events were isolated events and therefore of less concern. Perhaps the worker was afraid of the fuss my mother and her drinking buddies would make should she try to remove us. I don't have the answer however, all I can do is speculate.

It was at this time I met Jane, as well as another worker from the CAS. I didn't realise how important Jane would become in my life, not then. The only thing on my mind was the anxiety I felt about being placed in my next foster home. I crossed my fingers and hoped that my sister and I wouldn't end up back at the Grippen's.

But the Lake's were different, right from the start. They had a house full of kids and a warm welcome for us. I felt comfortable calling them mom and dad from the day we arrived. They lived on a farm and there were many animals and of course lots of chores and things to do. It took quite some time to develop trust, but surprisingly I settled in well with this family. They were good people who genuinely loved the many kids they cared for. I spent a long time wondering when and who I would be sexually abused by. Would it be the father, or the two older brothers? Thankfully, nothing ever happened to me there. As the days turned into weeks and I remained safe, I truly settled in and began relaxing and for the first time, just being a kid.

The four years I was with the Lake's were the most normal years I experienced as a child. I played outside, had fun, made friends and just did kid stuff. With three foster sisters, I had instant friends and of course someone to fight with.

Sometimes when the kids and I fought they would make fun of me and the stories I told of my life before coming to live with them. They thought it was funny when I told them that I could just open a can of Campbell's soup and eat it with a spoon, or that you could make soup with a can of cream corn. I tried to tell them that if you are hungry enough it tastes pretty good that way.

The Lake's made it clear to all of us that there were no bad kids, just bad parents. This provided me with a sense of security and it took some of the pressure off living in a foster home. I remember one day, after I had been there a while, I was doing some yard chores with Mr. Lake. He was showing me how to use the lawn mower and I blurted out, "I can't do that." He carefully explained to me that there was no such thing as can't. I tried to come up with a list of things I couldn't do, but it seemed that he had a reasonable and simple solution to each "can't" that I came up with. The list of problems has slipped from my memory, but what has stayed with me all these years, is that if you set your mind to it you can solve any problem.

Being the youngest of four girls, I was often trying to figure conversations out. When the conversation about periods came up, as it always does with girls, I asked for an explanation. Upon hearing the explanation I remembered the incident when I was eight, and told them that I had already had my period. This made everyone laugh as they explained that it isn't something that happens only once. I would be in my 30's before I fully understood that I had been sexually assaulted that night. I don't know if I was asleep or have blocked that event from memory. But to this day I cannot identify who my perpetrator was with absolute certainty.

Mrs. Lake was a stay at home mom, she had dinner on the table when we got off the school bus so we could eat before doing the farm chores. She always had time in the evenings to play games with us, the most popular being rummy at the kitchen table.

Not too long after arriving at the Lake's I began having dental problems. Dental care had not been a priority while living with my mother; surviving had been the priority. During dinner one evening I was unable to eat because of the pain I felt when anything touched my teeth. Jane arrived the following day to take me to the dentist. He diagnosed me with pyorrhoea and was quite concerned that I would lose all my teeth. I received medication and special toothbrushes and fortunately did not lose all my teeth.

While the Lake's provided me with stability for a period of time, longer than I had ever known, Jane would provide me with many of the skills required to build a life for myself. She was caring and non-judgemental, and she gave more of herself than the job required. I could not have reached this place in my life without the nurturing and love that she provided and still provides to this day. She was the queen of multi-tasking, which benefited those in her care, and she could always find the time to listen to you. Jane saw the good in everyone, and she believed in me. I have no doubt that is what allowed me to believe in myself and to make changes in my life when the opportunity arose. Jane was just my social worker and did not work with my family, they had their own worker. This helped strengthen the bond between Jane and I because I never had to worry that she was telling my mother about me.

Jane would laugh with me, and at me, and we always enjoyed the time we shared. She made me feel like I was the bright spot in her life, which is exactly how I felt about her. She was always optimistic and positive, making me feel like anything was possible. Her love for me was unconditional; she didn't take anything personally during the times when I was angry at her about my circumstances.

Jane was an excellent listener and always supportive, but was never the person who would say that I should do 'this' or 'that'. Rather, she would provide all the relevant information, and then without interference allow me to come up with my own conclusions. From there I could evaluate the options, and with her assistance (when needed) make the best decision. The advantage of this method is that I never felt embarrassed or ashamed to discuss any of my plans with her.

Jane always had positive words to say about me, and that slowly built my self-esteem. She told me I was insightful, smart, and funny. In my eyes Jane was my guardian angel, she took me from my nightmare and put me in a safe place.

She would also remind me of the good things in life. She helped me understand that my decisions alone would ultimately decide my future and the possibilities were endless. She talked to me as an equal, not just some 'bad' kid. This was very significant to me. It made me feel like my thoughts and ideas were very important.

During the first year at the Lake's, while the courts were trying to decide how they would proceed with my custodial arrangement, there was a family evaluation completed by the hospital. The report follows.

KINGSTON GENERAL HOSPITAL
Kingston, Ontario, Canada, K7L 2V7
Telephone 613-547-2121

Department of Psychiatry,
Juvenile Court Assessment Clinic
24 Barrie Street,

March 17, 1976.

Judge G. M. Thompson,
Juvenile and Family Court,
86 Clarence Street,
Kingston, Ontario

<u>*Re: Brenda Secor and Baby Sister*</u>

Dear Judge Thompson:

The following is the Clinic's recommendations with respect to these two children. You will recall that your referral addressed your concern that while the Children's Aid Society was asking for extensions of both the supervisor and temporary wardship orders, that the evidence you were hearing in the case lead you to wonder whether Baby Sister should perhaps be out of the home as well. You also hoped that a plan could be arranged with the Children's Aid Society which would protect both the children.

I have seen the parents on six occasions and Brenda on one occasion in the company of her family Social Worker. The family Social Worker and I have jointly participated in all these interviews and we have jointly participated in the development of the recommendations.

The parents have both been very cooperative about attending the Clinic. It would appear as I have gathered the information from them and from the Social Worker that the difficulties in this family have been long-standing in that the stability in the home has been tenuous over the last several years. By this I mean that there are a number of factors both social and emotional which have stressed this unit and have lead to intermittent episodic de-compensations on the part of either Wanda or Albert and have subsequently disrupted the family unit. Of particular concern here is the habitual and episodic drinking that both undertake during periods of increased stress. The Social Worker has seen the family through a number of these de-compensations and subsequent up-swings into relative stability. The Children's Aid Society and Your Honour have been concerned about the episodic drinking, and it must be clear that while this was immediately broached to the family as a concern, that they in fact do not see it as a major problem. Wanda has been an in-patient last summer at Dr. Lafferty's unit and remains in loose contact with the social worker there and in spite of this continues to have episodic drinking bouts. The drinking does seem to be tied to increased stress that either Wanda or Albert would undergo, either in relation to tensions between the two of them, or social and economic pressures. It would be my impression that tensions within the family, such as in the past between Wanda and Brenda, have also contributed to stress, drinking, and subsequent disruption of the family unit. Both Albert and Wanda acknowledge that when one of them is drinking the other one, in the past, has always remained sober to care for Baby Sister.

The recent home conditions which lead to the Court appearance have during the period of adjournment been rectified by the parents. Albert is usually unemployed during the winter months and then works as a carpenter during the rest of the year. In the context of this, a number of his relatives were using the home as a drinking place and when faced with the concerns of the Court and the possibility of removing Baby Sister, Albert successfully rectified these conditions and during the period of adjournment neither parent has come to attention with respect to drinking themselves. The Family Social Worker reports that she has been satisfied with the conditions of the home at the times that she has visited.

With respect to Baby Sister, I have certainly been aware of the concern that both parents have had over the possibility of losing her. In the interview situations they both actively parent and look after Baby Sister and seem truly fond of her. Baby Sister herself responds eagerly to both parents.

With respect to Brenda, the situation is more complicated. Brenda has been in care now for perhaps nine months and *essentially is doing very well in the foster-home setting. She still has a number of upsets, but these do not appear to get out of hand and it is clear that Brenda can be managed with firm limits. She is doing well in school. Wanda notes that the difficulty she saw in herself related to dealing with Brenda was that she found herself unable to be firm and to place controls and limits on Brenda, while Albert could. Wanda and Albert are clear that they would like Brenda to come home. Wanda is aware that there may be a reoccurrence of the difficulties that she had in managing Brenda and that bringing Brenda home will put stress on the family as they begin to adjust to each other again and see what problems there may be in the relationship. It is Wanda's hope that Brenda's period of time in care will have allowed her to change to the point where she is able to control herself and respond to Wanda's limits. Brenda herself would appear to be ambivalent about returning home. It is clear that when she is asked to choose that she would prefer to be at home, with the parents and Baby Sister whom she feels very close to. She also states that she would not want to be at the home if there was continued drinking. She has spoken with the Social Worker and indicated that if such problems were to arise again, that she would hope the Social Worker would take her back into care. Apparently with the individual Child Care Worker, Jane who supervises her placement, she talks a lot about the indecision of knowing where she is to be.*

In summary, we have a family that has a number of combined social – economic stresses and internal interpersonal problems which when combined lead to periods of disorganization, manifested in episodic drinking bouts in both the parents. There have been clear indications that the parents have responded to the external limits placed on them by the Court over the last six weeks and have performed most adequately during this period of time.

The recommendations are as follows:

1. *Baby Sister should continue to live with the parents under a continued supervisory order. I do not share the view that because Brenda is out of the home that Baby Sister should be out of the home as well. I think both children place different stresses on the family and that caring for Baby Sister is something that the family can do adequately. I recognize that one of the primary concerns – that of drinking – has not changed with respect to the assessment and would see only that continued supervision will help in detecting stresses as well as keeping the family directed towards behavior that would not lead to concerns in the helping agencies.*

2. *Continued temporary wardship for Brenda in the context of a clear attempt to place her at home at this point in time on a trial basis. What the Social Worker*

and I have in mind here is based on the fact that we feel we cannot adequately tell the Court at this point in time whether or not the family situation will break down once again, or whether there have been sufficient changes to allow them to function more stably. During the period of Society wardship, Brenda has only been home for weekends which really gives no clear indication of the relationships between Wanda and herself, and nor do they give each of them a chance to really try it out with each other again. We would suggest Brenda now be allowed to come home during reading week – March 20th to the 28th. We would plan to follow this up by an interview at the end of the period of time to look at and to review any problems that might have occurred. We would also hope that Brenda could come home perhaps the 1st of May for a period of a month and a half, during which time the Social Worker and I would actively follow the family in an attempt to assess and deal with any of the problems that might occur. I think this is the only way that we will adequately know whether or not a return placement at home will work and also the only way that Brenda and her mother can get a feel of whether or not this will work. We would recommend then that a wardship hearing be set for some time in mid-June. The Social Worker will be in touch with Brenda's school to ascertain whether or not this will interfere with a placement for her in a Grade 6 class next September. My impression is that, based on her marks to-date, this decision probably would not be effected by bring her out of her current school placement shortly before the end of the year.

I have discussed these recommendations with Albert and Wanda and they are both in agreement. I have not had a chance to discuss this with Brenda.

Yours truly,
James S. M.D., F.R.C.P. (c).
Director
c.c Children's Aid Society

Although the judge did take the time to ask me some questions and listen to my concerns, I, being pretty young at the time, was never made privy to the psychiatric department's findings.

Meanwhile at the Lake's, I went to school and lived a somewhat normal life. I didn't want to go home with my mother, but my little sister didn't have a choice, so home she went. She came back to visit a few times and this was very upsetting for the Lake's as they were sad to see her go back to the life I described to them. They may have been providing some kind of relief care, or perhaps it was intended to provide me with an opportunity to see my little sister. When it was time for my sister to leave she would be crying because she wanted to stay. The Lake's would also be very upset, and I was sad to see her go. I was very worried about my little sister, as I had been her main caregiver back home when everyone else was too drunk.

I remember speaking to the judge privately and telling him I did not want to go home unless my mother quit drinking and Albert was gone. He was mean to me and I didn't trust him. When the judge told this to my mother she said she had tried to raise one child without a father, but wasn't going to raise my baby sister without one. Following the hearing I was made a ward of the Crown, but my sister unfortunately went back to my mother, and Albert.

IN THE PROVINCIAL COURT (FAMILY DIVISION) FOR
THE COUNTY OF FRONTENAC
His Honour Judge G. M. Thomson   July 30th, 1976

I N T H E M A T T E R O F :

THE CHILD WELFARE ACT

And

BRENDA SECOR

B E T W E E N :

THE CHILDREN'S AID SOCIETY OF

THE CITY OF KINGSTON,

Applicant

Vs

WANDA AND ALBERT

Respondents

A P P E A R A N C E S :

Lawyer 1   for Brenda Secor

Lawyer 2   for Wanda

Lawyer 3   for Albert

I have reviewed the evidence in this matter and I have reached a decision that the child, Brenda Secor, is a child in need of protection and that she should be made a ward of the Crown. Unlike the case of Baby Sister, I feel that her situation is such that even a marked improvement in Wanda's circumstances would make the full-time return of Brenda impossible. In particular, I would note the following factors regarding Brenda:

1. *The relationship between Brenda and her mother has deteriorated to the point where it is not possible for them to live together for any length of time. I think this has been amply demonstrated by the evidence regarding visits home as well as the evidence as to the circumstances surrounding apprehension.*

2. *Wanda herself has expressed the viewpoint that she is unable to control Brenda, and I feel that she evidenced a strong apprehension about the possibility of having Brenda back at home. Her wish to have the child returned seems to be premised primarily upon the hope the past difficulties will somehow disappear almost immediately.*

3. *Brenda has been in care for over a year, with visits home having gone very badly. If she were not made a Crown ward, I think we would realistically be facing a further*

extension of temporary wardship. In my view, the child ought not to be left in this state of limbo any longer. I think it is clear that the uncertainty of her position is having its effect upon her.

4. *Brenda is not the natural child of Albert and the relationship between her and Albert is not a close one. This distinguishes her markedly from Baby Sister.*

5. *Because of her age, Brenda has faced the chaos of her home for a much longer period, has been more extensively affected by it, and thus is more in need of a guaranteed stability as soon as possible.*

In my decision with respect to Baby Sister, I noted the evidence of long-term instability within this family which rendered the children in need of protection. The evidence did not disclose that the younger child had, as yet, suffered extensively as a result of this and there is some prospect for future improvement on the part of the parents. As a result, I returned that child, subject to Children's Aid Society supervision. With Brenda there is clear evidence that she has been adversely affected by the events of the past and she has been out of the home for some time with little real hope of successful reintegration in the near future. Extensive efforts have been made in the past to rehabilitate this family, particularly during the early part of this year. In the case of Brenda, I feel that the recent improvement on the part of Wanda is too little, too late. Continued temporary wardship would be of little value in determining this child's ability to return home on a full-time basis and would certainly be damaging to the child herself. Accordingly, I have decided to make her a Crown ward as of today's date.

Two further matters concern me. One is that I am effectively separating the two children. I am unhappy about this but I feel the different circumstances of the two children justify this result. As well, I note that Brenda has survived well over a year when the contact between the two children has been slight.

Secondly, I have given a great deal of thought to the question of whether I should attach an access order to the order of Crown Wardship. This would be in recognition that there will always be an emotional tie between Brenda and her mother which should be faced and maintained as constructively as possible. Counsel for the child suggested this as a possibility so that Brenda could remain in the foster home on a long-term basis and could maintain some contact with her mother with the possibility of future return if Wanda's condition should improve for a substantial period of time.

In a sense the access order would recognize the risks involved in attempting adoption placement at this stage of the child's life.

I have decided not to make an access order. I feel that this would unduly restrict the agency in its plans for Brenda. As well, I think this would further confuse the child and create an unwarranted expectation in the mother of return to the home in the near future. However, I would ask the agency to consider the bonds which have developed over the past years, despite the chaotic home environment, when making its future plans for Brenda.

Provincial Judge

Once I was Crown ward there were different goals and challenges for everyone involved. I was happy at the Lake's, although I occasionally wished for a mother of my own who would take me shopping or treat me as someone special. Luckily, Jane took over that role. She always took me for ice cream when we had appointments, and thought it was hilarious how I could get so much ice cream all over me. I loved her dearly and appreciated the time she spent with me.

I was on cloud nine when she talked about adopting me. I would have the opportunity to be a part of a family and especially to have her all to myself. It was going to be awesome, I would be the happiest kid in the world. She just needed some time to think about it and talk to her partner, and her superiors at work.

But then, I should have known better than to get my hopes up. After thinking about it, Jane let me know that she couldn't adopt me, because she didn't feel she would be able to tell me "NO". Of course I thought if I was good enough for long enough, she will see that she won't ever have to tell me "NO". I didn't realize at the time how difficult it must have been for Jane to remain my social worker rather than my parent.

During my time in foster care I was placed with adoptive parents twice. The first time was shortly after becoming a Crown ward. William and Helen Smith lived in South River a little community outside of North Bay. They were both high school teachers and had two sons. Bobby was a year older than I was and Randy was a year younger, so I fit perfectly in the middle. They came to the Lake's visiting me and all the farm animals. It did seem strange to be spending time with my new 'family' since I actually liked the foster family I had. While I understood that foster families are temporary, it wasn't easy to think about leaving the only stability I had known in my life.

I went to spend the March break with the Smith's and moved in with them a short time after that. I remember wondering on the drive from Kingston to South River how much they had paid for me. I thought about asking Jane this question but was worried that she would say they had not paid very much for me. You could say that every time I was moved my low self-esteem would surface.

That issue all but disappeared once I was back in school, everyone was so friendly. The kids were accepting and I fit in without any problems. I quickly made a couple of friends who were interested in knowing more about me. It felt like I was living in a fairy tale. How could everything be so great for everyone, when I felt so out of place? Nothing was familiar, not even the school work. And why were all these people who don't even know me going out of their way to be so nice to me? The teachers all knew me by name and would say, "Hi" in the halls as I passed and yet I was wound up tight waiting for the other shoe to drop. I was sure I couldn't live up to the expectations that the whole community seemed to have of me.

When I found out that Helen and William's sister and brother were watching to see how it all turned out, as they were thinking of adopting a kid as well, I felt an unbearable sense of responsibility. So I guess it is not surprizing that I began to turn the Smith's life upside down. Bobby was a good kid, he was kind and accepting of me. But I was suspicious. I mean if I were him I sure wouldn't want to share my parents with a new kid.

The Smith's purchased all kinds of new furniture, clothes and toys for me. I asked Bobby if this made him jealous and he said no because he knew I needed these things. He had given up his bedroom and now shared one with his brother, so that I could have his room. It was filled with new stuff, and I watched Bobby carefully, but I have to admit that he didn't act very jealous.

It's very unfortunate that the Smith's didn't know much about my background before I came to live with them; however, since I'd told very little to anyone, they really had no way of knowing. I'm also not sure if anyone had told them how difficult the transition period could be. I think they truly believed I could just move in and live happily ever after. Instead I had loud and demanding tantrums, like I hadn't had since I lived with my mother. I guess it was a way to relieve some of the stress I felt because I wasn't sure what I was supposed to do at times. Whether it be real or imagined, it felt like the Smith's had high expectations of me. It ws just a matter of time before I snapped and failed. I am pretty sure they had never experienced anything like me in their entire lives.

As with most kids there were power struggles. When there was an after school teacher meeting, we got home before Helen and William, and the rule was that Bobby was in charge because he was the oldest. I felt this was unfair as he was only one year older than me and shouldn't always get to be in charge.

I also challenged the Smith's authority as parents. On Friday nights we went into North Bay to get groceries for the week, and this trip included dinner at McDonalds. The drive to and from North Bay was about an hour each way, so we would arrive home on Friday nights between 8:30 and 9:00 which was our bed time. I argued that this was unfair, as we didn't have time to watch any TV or do anything we wanted. I thought our bed time should be later on Fridays. Eventually I won this battle and Friday night bedtime was extended to 10:00.

William enjoyed playing with the children and thought nothing of bouncing me on his knee. I however, was uncomfortable with this as I had seen how similar games turned out in the past. The harder William tried to be a good parent and show me lots of affection, the more I screamed and demanded that Helen take his place. If I was sick William rubbed Vicks on my chest, or brought me medicine. I wanted Helen to do these things with me and the more I demanded the farther she retreated from me. This of course made me very angry, because I only wanted her to spend time with me and she didn't seem to want to.

Helen truly felt that because I didn't have a good relationship with my mother, I would be unable to develop one with her. In fact, the opposite was true. I feel that had I been able to secure her attention and build a relationship with her, things would have turned out differently.

Instead, I felt pretty sure that Helen was not very interested in me. When she did anything with me, it seemed more for William's sake than mine. When I first arrived to live with William and Helen they told me that if my little sister became a Crown ward they would consider adopting her as well. After living with Helen and William for a few weeks I asked if they were still going to adopt my sister when she came into care. They said that she was too young, they worked full time and wouldn't be able to care for her during the day.

I was now feeling like they were lying to me they told me before I came that if my sister became a ward they would adopt her also. Trust is a big issue for a child even in the best of times. Every day my trust of this new life was diminishing. Other misunderstandings arose over silly things. Bobby and I were playing with some friends in the field across from the house and he ended up sitting on me and I was unable to get up. He then proceeded to threaten to kiss me and in response I spit in his face. Although I may have been abused by adults, I sure wasn't about to be abused by someone my own age. In hindsight and in fairness to Bobby, whose upbringing was normal, the incident was innocent and non-threatening. None-the-less William and Helen were not happy, and at that age I certainly couldn't find the words to explain why I wasn't about to let my brother kiss me.

Finally, during a tantrum I threatened to leave – at which time Helen packed my bags and called the local social worker. I waited for her out on the grass in the front yard, devastated. Sad that I had threatened to leave and sad that they were so happy to agree. I felt responsible for everyone's disappointment, as I was aware they were very sad as well. I did my best to convince them that maybe it was just me, and they would perhaps like my former foster sister Janet much better. After all she was much quieter and nicer than I was. However, they were soured on the idea of adoption and I felt guilty that I had spoiled not only their hopes for adoption, but the possibility that their brother and sister might adopt too.

What follows are two letters written between the local director of Parry Sound Children's Aid Society (near where the Smith's lived) and the Executive Director of Frontenac County Children's Aid Society (where I used to live with my mother).

From the Children's Aid Society's (CAS) perspective, the two letters explain the relationship I had with the Smiths, and why the CAS felt this relationship failed.

Jane worked for the Frontenac County CAS.

Mr. David Badlock,
Local Director,
Children's Aid Society of the
District of Parry Sound,
76 Church Street,
Parry Sound, Ontario
P2A 1Z1

April 12, 1977

<u>Attention: Amy Lewis</u>

Re: Brenda Secor
And
William and Helen Smith

Dear Mr. Badlock:

Brenda was placed with Mr. and Mrs. Smith on April 11, 1977. We would appreciate it if you would accept supervision of this placement and bill us at your usual per diem rate.

Brenda appeared to be quite happy about being adopted by the Smith's. She seems to have made a commitment to these people. She did express some concern that she would not see her foster family, the Lake's again but both the worker and the Smith's assured her that she would be allowed to visit.

Although Brenda and the Smith's appear to care for each other very much the worker feels that there may be some problems. Brenda informed the worker that the Smith's thought of returning her to Kingston during the visit which began March 31, 1977. Although the family seem to have worked this out, it certainly aroused a sense of insecurity and doubt in Brenda. She felt that the Smith's expected everything to go beautifully with only minor problems where Brenda was prepared for real adjustments.

She also expressed fear that the boys, would only have to fight with her to threaten her position in the family. The worker feels that Brenda will need much reassurance and will be slower to trust because of the incident. Brenda does not expect to be accepted immediately as a daughter but she does expect this feeling to develop within the family. She states that she was "kind of scared" that the Smith's would never see her as being their own. She understands that this feeling will take some time to grow and the worker feels, is somewhat frightened that the family may give up too soon.

The Smith's seemed to have some trouble in relating to the very mature and very childish behaviour that Brenda exhibits. They seemed to find it difficult to adjust to her lapses into near baby talk as well as her clear-eyed, realistic outlook. The worker explained that Brenda had been a mother to her sister for some time and missed a good deal of mothering of her own. She is a very warm and loving girl who likes to be cuddled. She also likes to be treated as a person in her own right with respect given to her ideas and feelings. The Smith's are a very warm and open family and have a lot of positive to offer this placement. However, the worker has one concern. Both Mr. and Mrs. Smith have expressed a belief that "fate" will have a great deal to do with the success or failure of this placement. The worker is concerned that an attitude of "what will be, will be" may jeopardize this adoption. We hope that the Smith's realize that adoption, like any developing relationship, does not just happen but must be worked at. The worker is concerned that they may feel that the problem between them and Brenda has been resolved with one discussion. Brenda is aware that there will be many problems before the family unit is tied together and we hope the Smith's are also aware that problems may reoccur. They did not seem to expect the boys to have any problems in coping with their new sister and were very worried when one came up. We realize that both the Smith's have been under a great deal of pressure concerning this placement and may have been overreacting due to this pressure. Basically, we have very positive feelings about this placement. The Smith's with their openness and warmth, have much to offer a child like Brenda. And Brenda, with her realism and honesty, has much to offer the Smith's.

Jane mentioned that Brenda had told her in confidence that her step-father had tried to molest her when she was about five. We have no information concerning this.

In conclusion we would like to say that we feel this placement has great potential. We do feel that Brenda was more aware of the realities of adoption placement than the Smith's. We feel that this may cause some problems in that Brenda's expectations for herself and the family are not as high as those of the Smith's. We hope that any future problems can be dealt with positively.

We hope we have expressed our concerns clearly. Thank you for your co-operation and we look forward to getting reports on the progress of this placement.

Yours sincerely,

D. A. Sudd,

Executive Director.

Frontenac County Children's Aid Society

DISTRICT SOCIAL SERVICES

THE CHILDREN'S AID SOCIETY
DISTRICT OF PARRY SOUND
76 CHURCH STREET
REPLY TO THE ATTENTION OF
A. LAWSON   June 1, 1977

Mr. D. A. Sudd,
Executive Director,
Frontenac County Children's Aid Society,
Box 357, 173 Princess St.,
Kingston, Ont.

Attention: Ms. Jane

Dear Mr. Sudd:

Re: Brenda Secor and

William and Helen Smith

As you are aware, the adoption of Brenda by the Smith family has ended unsuccessfully and we would like to outline for you here the stages the placement went through and the deterioration of the relationships involved.

The Smith's felt very positive about both visits with Brenda prior to placement. They were excited, pleased and anxiously anticipating incorporating Brenda into their family. As mentioned in your letter on April 12, there had been disagreements, particularly between Brenda and the oldest son during the visit, but the Smith's felt at that time, that the problems were not insurmountable.

The worker's initial visits with Brenda were fairly superficial, as Brenda would admit to no problems in the home, and would become quite closed when discussing these issues. She subsequently opened up more, and it became obvious that she had thought of the worker as the Smith's worker, rather than hers. After this admission, she was much more open.

Problems in the home began cropping up almost immediately. Brenda was quite defiant, talked back, accused favouritism, and on occasion had temper tantrums.

The Smith's were puzzled by some of the behaviour as Brenda, herself, admitted that this was not normal behaviour for her. The worker feels the turning point of the placement came after an incident which required the worker's immediate involvement, requested by the family. At that point the Smith's were feeling extremely discouraged but after a family conference, it was agreed that all parties would make an extra attempt to have the placement work. Brenda's behaviour improved considerably over the next ten days or so, although the worker feels the Smith's were waiting for another issue to crop up. The worker feels the family had perhaps given up prior to this good week, and that they were just biding time, knowing already that the placement was to be unsuccessful. The final issue came up when the Smith's wanted to discuss an incident with Brenda, and she refused to talk, She called the worker at this point, feeling betrayed, as she had made a real attempt and felt they did not appreciate her efforts. The worker agreed to see the entire family the next day. In the meantime, apparently Brenda accused Mr. Smith of being a liar (saying he felt her behaviour had improved, and then stating that he did not feel things were going well) and it was at this point the Smith's decided they felt the placement could not possibly work. They discussed this with Brenda, who became quite upset, and refused to stay with them the night. They had been looking at the possibility of carrying on at least until the end of the school year, but apparently Brenda would not go to bed, and thus the Smith's brought her to the worker's home. The Smith's had made up their minds at this point, and could not see any point in trying to prolong the issue. Brenda still did not want to go, and felt all her efforts to improve had been in vain. The parting was not fiery, but was one of outward affection. Brenda showed her upset only briefly.

The Smith's feel that the basic problem was one of conflicting personalities. They were upset that her behaviour was obviously so much worse in their home than it was anywhere else – wondering what was wrong that would cause this. They found that Brenda was constantly trying to play one parent off against the other, and one of the boys off against the other. While Brenda was accusing them of favouritism, so, too were the boys accusing them of giving extra privileges to her. They felt there was a constant tension in the air that was playing on everyone's nerves, causing tempers to be short, and general emotional fatigue. The greatest cause for alarm was that they felt relationships were deteriorating rather than improving, and that Brenda was growing farther from them all the time.

The worker feels a part of the problem was that the Smith's expectations of success far exceeded the time limit they were allowing. No child's behaviour is going to mold into a new family in such a short time span, yet they felt more changes should have occurred. The parent is boss in the Smith household, and is expected to be respected. Brenda was rude, defiant, talked back, etc., and this was not acceptable over a long period of time. A lot of Brenda's behaviour was obviously testing, and feeling out of her new position; although the worker, too, wonders why her behaviour was apparently so much worse than any displayed in the past. Brenda does demand a lot of attention; a fact which prompted the Smith's to suggest she be placed in a childless family, should she be placed for adoption again. Brenda does not want this.

The Smith's do not plan to adopt another child; primarily because of the severity of the emotional drain that has occurred within their family. Apparently when they told Brenda this, she said that they should as there were several little girls at Lake's that were much better behaved than she was. Brenda also told the worker that she knew from the start that adoption would not work, and used some of the children at Lake's as examples to prove her point. She seemed to react as though she knew the whole thing was inevitable.

In conclusion, we would like to express our sincere regret that the proposed adoption was unsuccessful, and hope that Brenda will be able to readjust to her situation there.

Yours truly,

D. J. Badlock,
Local Director,
The Children's Aid Society
Parry Sound, Ontario

Reading these letters helped me deal with my past. Doing so alleviated some of the guilt that I felt around this period of my life and helped me recognize that I was not the only one to blame. Regrettably the Smith's were not very well prepared for the transition of adding an older child to their family. For what I thought were good reasons, I know I pushed the boundaries. But given my background I had reasoned it was easier to do the rejecting than be rejected. Unfortunately the Smith's were never given guidance on how to accept and work with a child who was the victim of rejection.

After my first adoption failure with the Smith's, I returned to Frontenac County and for awhile continued to live with the Lake's. When I returned to school I was disappointed to have the same teacher as when I had left. We hadn't gotten along too well the first time. However, something had changed for one or both of us, because she was the best teacher I ever had. I was very sad to see her leave our school at the end of Grade 6. She had been very supportive and encouraging since my return.

Shortly after my return, the Lake's began to have problems. They started drinking all the time and they started to fight; Mr. Lake even began to threaten violence against his wife. It felt like I had been here before. I started feeling depressed and lonely and I realized it was only a matter of time before I moved on again.

In the summer following Grade 6, I went through another trial adoption. This family lived in Kingston, which meant I could visit them regularly 'to test the waters' before moving in. At this point I had started to periodically see my own mother again. I would spend one weekend a month with her, even though she never acted happy to see me. She always reminded me not to drink the milk, as it was for my sister and she didn't have any money to buy more.

In contrast, I liked hanging out with Dan and Fran, my new potential family. Sometimes Fran seemed distant, maybe because she had to work when I visited in the summer. I think Dan, was a pastor at a church, and had more time.

I enjoyed hanging out with Dan and never felt threatened or vulnerable at any time. We would often play chess and he would teach me some great moves. We went sailing on his sailboat, and swimming at Fort Henry. There was a certain calmness or peacefulness from Dan that just rubbed off on me as I hung around him. I also worried that if the placement didn't succeed it would be too much for me to handle. While I was content hanging out with Dan, I was never quite sure if Fran liked me or not. Sometimes Jane and I would spend an afternoon doing crafts with Fran, but I don't think I ever spent time with Fran alone.

I felt that if your own mother didn't love you, there must be something wrong with you. Mothers have to love their children, right? So if a mother didn't love her child there must be something really wrong with the child. I figured it was just a matter of time before everyone else figure out something was wrong with me too, and then they would reject me. I had learned it was easier to do the rejecting, and to do it before becoming attached. But I was extremely worried that if I said I didn't want to be adopted, I would spoil it for Dan and Fran.

Eventually I felt comfortable enough during a chess game to ask Dan if they might try adopting another child, if it didn't work out with me. Dan said of course they would, and I was hugely relieved as this answer provided me with an out. Had he said no, I think I would have followed through with this adoption due to the guilt I felt over the first failed adoption. Instead, I told Jane that I didn't want to be adopted and would like to remain in contact with my own mother. Although I only spent a short time with him, in later years I would fully appreciate the value of the time I spent with Dan.

I continued to live with the Lake's and to visit my mother and sister occasionally. The tensions increased at the Lake's when Mr. Lake had lost his job, and they both started drinking even more. CAS eventually removed all the children from the home, except for me and another girl my age – we both refused to go. Our foster parents were angry and everyone involved was upset and blaming everyone else.

Jane was still my worker, but now my foster parents were furious with her. They blamed her for the children being removed, refusing to acknowledge that it was the drinking and chaos. I felt like I was being forced to choose between them. I had been at the Lake's for four years, and Jane had decided not to adopt me, even though I loved her so much and had been so good for the last two years. So the next time she showed up, I told her to go away and never come back. Seeing her just created problems with my foster parents anyway. Rejecting Jane made my foster parents love me again for the time being.

I started to smoke and drink at school and eventually started using drugs. Drugs were great because when I took them, nothing mattered. I didn't like alcohol but I could choke it down, as long as it helped me feel better. I started to do things like skip school and hitchhike into Kingston for the day; shoplifting was a cool way to make money. On school trips I would take everyone's requests for items, which I would then steal and sell to them cheap. I would say I was staying overnight at a friend's house and then spend the weekend in Kingston at a friend's uncle's place, and party all weekend long.

Another time, Janet, my foster sister and I ran away from school. We were making our way to Kingston to find Jane. I am pretty sure that we were reacting to the stress at home. We didn't hitchhike, because we were afraid of getting picked up by someone who knew us. The Lakes came looking for us and we ended up hiding in the ditch while they stood on the road calling our names.

This roller coaster continued until my foster parents decided that they were going to move out west, with their children and Janet. They asked me to go with them. That caught me completely off balance. I had just started to visit my mother and sister again after two failed adoption attempts. Albert was no longer with my mother and if I chose to go with the Lake's I'd be leaving my mother again just when she might need me. And they were going so far away that I wouldn't be able to visit. So despite everything that had happened, I decided that I couldn't leave my mother.

I have looked for Janet for more than 20 years now and have been unable to find her. I hope that she is well because it makes me sad to think that something may have happened to her and no one noticed.

The Lake's had a huge garage sale to sell everything they weren't taking with them, and the other kids gave me the things they didn't have room for. Spin city, again! I spent my time doing all the drugs I could get, and I started to run away, as I couldn't stand to watch them pack up and leave me. Even though I had chosen to stay, I felt like I was being reminded that I didn't really belong anywhere or to anyone.

Fear seems to have always been a big, really big, part of my life. And my biggest fear has always been that no one will ever want me.

I ran away from the Lake's in October 1979, just when they were getting ready to leave me behind. The trigger was an argument over being able to use the phone. I stayed in a friend's garage for two days, before I was picked up at school and placed in the CAS Receiving Home in Kingston. I asked to have Jane back as my worker, which was the first positive thing I had done in a while. I had really missed Jane. I was enjoying the freedom of the Receiving Home, which is where they place children who don't have foster families. I was there for about two weeks and I was allowed to go out when I wanted as long as I was back by curfew. I loved being in town and I asked Jane not to place me in the country again, as there was nothing to do in the country.

However, I was placed in a new foster home in the country, maybe because it allowed me to continue classes in my old high school or perhaps they didn't have anything in the city to offer. I stayed in this foster home for a couple of months, and during that time, I got into every kind of trouble I could get into. One night, while everyone was out doing various things, dates, hockey games etc., I was so depressed (imagine) I sat on the top of the fridge and emptied all the pill bottles. I didn't know what I was taking, but I figured if nothing else, I would sleep that night. The next morning was my morning to do breakfast dishes and I felt like shit and couldn't stop shaking. I was a mess and my older foster sister did the dishes for me. Outside the fresh air seemed to help somewhat, but I also had an exam to write at school. I was shaking too much to write. When I tried, my writing was illegible, so I just sat there until it was over and left.

While I was at this foster home, one of their previous foster children, Pauline, returned from Ottawa for a short visit. She and her daughter needed some place safe to stay, so that her boyfriend couldn't find her. Apparently he was very scary and abusive. While she was there she told my foster sister and I that if we ever needed a place to stay, we could always stay with her.

Although by February 1980 I had on paper spent six months in high school, I had been absent from more than 60 classes. Most of the time I was down at the point in Sydenham getting drunk or stoned. I didn't feel like I fit in anywhere, and I sure wasn't one of the cool kids. I was pretty sure that I was never going to belong anywhere and was very scared that I would be alone all my life. Maybe that is why in February 1980 a few months after my fourteenth birthday I hooked up with a friend and ran away to Ottawa.

RUNAWAY
14-18 years of age

When I ran away to Ottawa I went with Peggy, the friend who had helped me when I ran away from the Lake's. I had stayed in her garage for two days back then; the fact that she had helped me made us closer.

Peggy and I hitchhiked to Ottawa planning to stay with Pauline. She had offered me a place to stay, and I didn't have any reason to stay where I was. I don't think I had any long term plans, it was just something to do, and who knows maybe it would make people notice me.

We arrived at Pauline's mom's house and met her family. I would later learn that Pauline's mom thought she was Ma Barker with all her criminal children. Later that night Pauline's abusive boyfriend showed up for a visit. Peggy and I had gone to bed, mostly to stay out of the way. Pauline's boyfriend, Terry was bugging her and asked where the nice blonde went, referring to Peggy. Pauline wasn't too amused by this and asked if he wanted to take us home with him, to which he replied, "that sounds good to me."

So Pauline came upstairs and got us. And unbelievably, we got dressed came down stairs and left with him. Terry was one frightening looking person. He dressed completely in black; had a large unruly beard, and a peg leg. All that was missing was the parrot, the ship, and he'd be one scary looking pirate.

He took us to his apartment, and then left to go pick up his daughter. When he left I remember telling Peggy that if she got mixed up with him our agreement to stick together would be over, and she agreed. We fell asleep and woke up when Terry returned with his little three year old daughter, Lynn. It appeared Peggy and I had made the right decision when we left Pauline's.

Terry had returned to Pauline's, they had a big fight and Terry was about to leave with Pauline's brother Dave and Dave's wife, Ruth. But at the last minute, Pauline asked Terry to stay and talk. A wise move, as Dave and Ruth took a taxi home, then assaulted the taxi driver at their own front door and stole his money. They rushed into the house and pretended to be asleep when the police arrived. Given this crime, it was not surprising that they then assaulted the officers who tried to arrest them. Ruth was released and Dave was sentenced to a few years in prison.

Terry was freaked out by this and felt it was better if Peggy and I stayed at Ruth's house. We could help look after her children, and he was also worried about having two runaway teenage girls living in his apartment. He told us we were lucky it had worked out as it did, because if we had stayed at Pauline's house, her mother and brothers would have abused us and had us working on a corner.

This was all a big change from my previous four years in the country. To live in Ottawa I would have to learn a lot about survival and learn it quick.

Babysitting was about the only way for a 14 year old runaway to earn money. At times, just having tampons was a luxury. There was a lady living a couple of blocks away from Ruth, who asked me to babysit her son. I went to her house to meet her and she showed me around. In the living room of her apartment there was a big blood stain on the carpet. She told me this was where the Outlaws motorcycle gang had 'splashed' her previous babysitter. I wasn't going to go and babysit for her after discovering that splashed meant gang raped. Terry said that rather than lose out on the money I suggest she bring her son to his house to be babysat. She agreed, but never asked me to babysit again as I am pretty sure her plan wasn't just to have me babysit.

When unable to find a babysitting job, I started shoplifting again to earn my keep. I stole mostly groceries and jewellery to later sell and buy what I needed.

I had been in Ottawa a couple of weeks and Peggy and I had been staying with Ruth whose house was a big party place. She laughed when she caught her five year old smoking a joint even after she had told him not to. After the first few weeks Ruth made it clear that Peggy could stay with her, as she would be turning 16 in a couple of months. However, it would be almost 2 years until I was 16 and was legally able to work. Ruth said she couldn't support me for that length of time.

With no place to go and not being ready to return to Kingston, I took Terry up on his offer to stay with him. I would not recognize until much later that the next four years would be the toughest of my life. I figured nothing could be worse than the life I had already experienced. But I would spend the next four years in a constant state of fright or flight, and Terry would destroy the little bit of self-confidence that I had. It kept me thin, but it just about destroyed me as an individual.

I was 14 when I met Terry's daughter Lynn for the first time. She was a beautiful little three-year-old girl, who was terminally ill with cystic fibrosis. A little girl with no mother and an abusive father. When I met Lynn, she was completely bald on the top of her head but she had beautiful long blonde hair, everywhere else. I thought it must have been a medical side-effect, and asked about it. I learned that when Terry had seen Lynn kiss a little boy he had dragged her around by the hair on her head. Needless to say I was horrified that a little girl of three could be treated like that, and coming from an abusive childhood myself the need to protect this little girl was very strong.

So that's how my relationship with Terry began. Little did I realize, or for that matter accept at the time, that this first incident would be the start of four years of total and complete terror. At first I stayed for Lynn, and Terry seemed like a guy with a bit of a temper, but nothing that couldn't be handled. Lynn was so cute and behaved like the perfect child. I thought maybe someone had misunderstood what had happen to her hair. She was so good, her father couldn't possibly have gotten that mad at her to do what he did. Sometimes though when her father spoke to her, I would see the fear in her eyes. My heart felt so sad when I recognized the fear in her eyes. I knew I had to protect her.

Lynn's mother had left Terry and Lynn about a year and half before I met them, but I was totally unable to understand how a mother could leave her child. I asked Terry why Lynn's mother had just left her and of course he said she just ran off with someone else. This made me even more determined to protect this little girl and help make up for all that she didn't have. I could be the big sister who would look after her and love her. After living with Terry and Lynn for a couple of weeks my relationship with Terry became a romantic one.

The relationship was calm for a week or two, but the arguments soon started. Terry was easily angered. Nothing was ever the way he liked it, everything was wrong. I didn't cook very well, I didn't know how to clean and so on.

Soon arguments would begin over nothing – things like I didn't dry Lynn's hair well enough after her bath. For the first few weeks he was verbally abusive. I was a liar and a slut. I was using him so I didn't have to go home. I was stupid, not worth his time. Then I made the mistake of telling him that I was sexually abused as a child and this just gave him something else to use against me. That's just the way it worked with Terry. Tell him something about my past to elicit some understanding, and he would just twist things around to my disadvantage. I can still feel the fear and anxiety he instilled in me twenty-eight years after the fact.

At the end of the first month of my romantic relationship with Terry, I still thought it would get better. Sure, he was verbally aggressive and abusive, but I could help him change. He just had a hard time trusting me, but I could win that trust and love him more than he ever knew was possible. (I was 14 and naïve.) Then, in the middle of a loud and heated argument, I decided that I had had enough of the accusations and threats, so I screamed at Terry that I hated his guts. Bad move. I was standing in front of him at the time and he kicked me in the ribs knocking me across the room where I landed on my ass completely out of breath. Somehow, I really hadn't expected that reaction. I was crying from shock and pain, and said I was leaving. I told Terry I grew up watching my mother getting the crap kicked out of her on a regular basis. I sure wasn't planning on going down the same road. "Not me", I shouted at him. "I'm not going to stay here and take that kind of shit."

I ran out of the apartment and into the snowy night, still crying. Terry chased me and in no time had caught up with me. He told me how sorry he was, that I couldn't leave like this. Besides it was night and I had nowhere to go. "Come back and stay till morning," he said. And of course he would not touch me again, at least not that night.

This scene, or very similar ones, would be repeated about a hundred times over the next four years. Each time we returned to the apartment Terry would say how sorry he was. But every time we had our differences he would over react, then physically take it out on me. It was no consolation to hear him say he was sorry after things like this happened, but that was the explanation I accepted. Things would always start all over again, and of course it would be my fault.

How could I forget Lynn? How could I want to leave that little girl who had started to love me like a mother? Wouldn't I feel bad earning her trust and then just leaving her like her mother did, without even a goodbye. Shame on me.

From then on fights occurred daily. I never did anything right or well enough. I was too stupid to think. I was a slut, lazy, useless. Terry was insanely jealous. If any man looked at me, it was my fault, because I was teasing and enticing him. Broads like me were a dime a dozen, he said. Sex was a humiliating experience, but of course you treat a slut like a slut. I often had a black eye: every week, every day was a nightmare. I felt very trapped.

Terry started drinking first thing in the morning and I never knew what was going to set him off. Sometimes I could talk him down, before things got out of hand and I didn't get so hurt. I learned that it didn't matter how hard I tried he would always find something to get angry about. The hard part was never knowing what would set him off, and even though it happened all the time, it often came as a sucker shot. Everything would appear to be fine, he seemed to be in a good mood, and then bang, I get punched in the face.

He actually thought my shock was funny. It proved how freaking stupid I was, that I didn't even know what he was pissed about, and it wasn't his fault if I was dumb enough to believe it hadn't upset him just because he was smiling. Thinking about his style of grim humour just makes me nauseous now, but back then this had become a daily pattern by the sixth month of our relationship.

That was when I made my first serious attempt to leave. I returned to Kingston and stayed at the Receiving Home. I had a visit with Jane who took me shopping since I didn't have any clothes. While I had been gone I would occasionally call Jane. I would tell her I was a live-in babysitter and to stop looking for me.

My stay at the Receiving Home grew old quick as I didn't want to follow any rules. The last thing I wanted was to be told what to do – this was what Terry had been doing constantly for the last six months. I started to miss Terry and especially Lynn, I worried how she would survive, if I wasn't there to protect her. I started to feel that I had created a bad situation for her, leaving her to deal with Terry who would be furious that I left.

I also worried that I was pregnant. I was pretty sure that the CAS would take a baby away from a fourteen-year-old. I needed Terry to make sure no one would take my baby away from me. So I called him and he came and picked me up in Kingston. Terry was, as usual, very sorry. He said that now that I was pregnant, things were going to be different. I wanted so much for that to be true that I believed him. I convinced myself that this baby was going to make our relationship better, it was going to show Terry just how much I loved him.

I didn't go to the doctor right away because I was a runaway and still only 14. Shortly after my fifteenth birthday, at six months pregnant, I made a doctor's appointment and changed my date of birth from 1965 to 1964, so I could pretend to be 16. The doctor was cold and aloof. I didn't have to guess that he disapproved of me having a baby, because he told me so.

Terry had gone right back to being abusive, but I still hoped that once the baby arrived he would change. Instead of making him happy, my pregnancy was another reason for him to be angry with me. Somehow it was all my fault that he was not only guilty of harbouring a 15 year-old runaway, but also guilty of statutory rape. Things would be less stressful when I was 16, he assured me. I convinced myself that if I just made it through the six months to my next birthday things would change. That's what he promised.

On April 6, I had a beautiful baby girl, Janie. The nurses gave me a hard time – How was I going to care for a child? Where would I live? They scared me to death and again I needed Terry. He pretended to be the good uncle who was going to look after his niece and her new baby and the nurses backed down a bit. I still thought about leaving, but with nowhere to go and no one to help, it was difficult to know how I was going to look after myself and a tiny baby.

Terry was smart enough to sense when I was thinking about leaving. Before I went into hospital, he went through my bag to see what I had packed and decided that I had packed too much for a couple of days in the hospital. He was suspicious and although I lied, and said I didn't plan on leaving, he insisted on making me leave the hospital one day before Janie could leave. That way when I picked up the baby I would have no clothes or personal items with me.

The next day he had a friend drive me to the hospital to pick up Janie. I had instructions to take a taxi home, but no money. He would pay the taxi upon my arrival. I went to the hospital, played with Janie, and dressed her while the nurses all said how strong and amazing she was at three days old. The whole time I was trying to think where I could go and how I could keep my baby safe and with me. I was still a runaway with no family or friends; I didn't have any money and in the end the only option I could see was to call a taxi and return to Terry with my baby.

When Janie was two weeks old, I was feeding her at the kitchen table and Terry was making coffee. The dishes from the night before hadn't been dried and put away, they were still in the dish tray. Terry picked up a casserole dish for closer inspection and deciding that it wasn't clean enough, he hit me on top of the head with it while I was holding the baby. Glass shattered everywhere and all I could do was yell at Terry to watch the baby. He took her from me and said she was fine.

Lynn and Janie became his personal weapons against me. If I told Lynn she couldn't do something, I was just picking on her because she wasn't mine. If I didn't scold Lynn, then I didn't love her because she wasn't mine. Lynn was often forbidden to speak to me, and he would threaten to hit her if she did. Janie, on the other hand, was Terry's little princess. Lynn and I could never please him, but Janie could never anger him. I had told him if he ever treated Janie like he treated Lynn and me, I wouldn't hesitate to leave. Maybe he believed that one threat, I don't know. But for

Janie's first three years Terry never hit her or yelled at her. The first time he slapped her was a couple of months before we left for the last time.

Janie was the only bright spot in my life, and Terry knew it. He told me he would never let me take Janie away, and he said his first wife didn't take Lynn because he had threatened to kill her and her whole family if she ever tried. I had no doubt that his first wife believed every word. If I tried to take Janie away, he would find us. It wasn't like we had anywhere to go, or anyone to protect us.

I was often terrified, and never knew what to expect. Sometimes Terry threatened to drag me down to The Outlaws club house to be splashed, just because the look of terror on my face made him laugh his ass off. There was the constant and continued threat of violence. Having other people around was no protection, he had no problem punching or kicking me in front of them. For me this just added to the humiliation. Bad enough to be hit in private, but when he hit me in front of other people I always believed they would think I was an ass for taking it.

A little after Janie was born, the apartment on the second floor of the house we were renting became available and Terry wanted to move upstairs. I had stopped expecting Terry to change and I didn't want to live at the top of stairs I would inevitably be thrown down. Of course we ended up moving upstairs, and it was exactly as I had imagined.

Terry started to have his friends over a lot, and was doing speed on a regular basis. When no one else was around to shoot it for him, I had to do it. I tried to explain that needles scared me, but as usual he won and I end up inserting needles in his veins.

There were nights when I lay in bed, thinking about the knives in the kitchen. But I knew that if I missed, I'd be dead myself. I played the scene over and over in my head, but always came to the conclusion that he was much bigger and stronger than I was. That is probably the only thing that saved him.

The summer after Janie was born, we got a Doberman pup. Terry had him house trained in record time and the dog listened well. Like the humans in the family, Dion learned to obey Terry. As Dion got bigger, Terry got more and more abusive towards him. By the time Dion was nine months he was as terrified of Terry as the rest of us. He would come when Terry called, but he would crawl on his stomach and lose control of his bowls as he inched forward. Of course, Terry, was disgusted by this 'wimpy' dog, and he would beat him even more.

I felt bad for Dion, but if Terry was beating on the dog it meant that he was leaving us alone at least for a short period of time. Now thinking of that dog breaks my heart and I wish I had done something for him. In the end Terry beat Dion to death and left him to die a slow death. Terry was in a rage and he and the dog were in the back yard. He kicked the dog in the head with his peg leg until both of the dog's eyes were bright red with blood. I think Terry realized that he may have over done it and he gave the dog away to the guy down the street. Dion died two days later.

When Terry went out drinking with his biker friends it was a mini holiday for the girls and me. We could play games and I could go to bed when they did and get some sleep. When Terry returned home at three or four in the morning, he would get me up to make him a fried egg sandwich, and his fun would begin. On one particular morning he brought his friend Bob home with him. I made the sandwiches and everyone was about to go to bed when Terry decided to check in on Lynn and noticed that she wasn't under her sheet, but only the blanket. He went into a rage about what a lazy useless slut I was, how could I not know she wasn't under her sheet?

I don't know why this humiliation was the turning point, but I knew I had to get out. I waited until Terry and Bob fell asleep, packed up what I could carry for Janie and left. When I was down the street a few blocks I asked to use someone's phone and called Interval House. I stayed at Interval House for two days, but I couldn't deal with the rules and the other women in the house continually teasing me about how there should be two cribs in my room, one for the baby and one for me. After two days, Terry didn't look so bad. I talked to him on the phone and of course he was sorry, he would make it up to me, just bring Janie home. And I did.

Around this time Terry decided to let Lynn's mother visit her, under his supervision of course. Martha (Lynn's Mother) came over to visit one Friday a month. This quickly became a drinking festival. Martha would arrive with bottles of alcohol and they would begin drinking. Terry criticized everything I did during these visits. I didn't get the drinks fast enough, I didn't talk enough and if I would drink I wouldn't have these problems. I had seen enough drunks to know that's not what I wanted to do or be, so I didn't start drinking even to please Terry.

Inevitably, one of these visits went especially bad and Terry beat me until I ran out the front door crying, with blood running down my face. As he chased me down Parkway Street, a bus pulled over to let me on. I had lost a shoe during the chase, and so there I was on the bus with one shoe, crying, embarrassed, bloody, with nowhere to go. I returned to Interval House and they gave me a pair of shoes. Back at that time they had a policy. If you stayed with them only to return to the same abusive relationship you had fled from, you could not stay with them again. So with two shoes, no money and nowhere to go, I walked across town to return home.

On another attempt to leave, I called Ottawa social services from a pay phone at three in the morning. I was told the intake worker would call me back, so I left the number of the pay phone. While I was waiting for the return call, a taxi pulled up on the street and asked if I needed a ride. I was still crying and upset but I explained that I was waiting for a phone call. He offered to take me to his sister's house, but I said I was going to wait for my phone call. After about 15 minutes he got out of the taxi and started talking a little more aggressively. I started to panic and tried to think what my options were, as I didn't like the way things were looking. Luckily, the phone rang as he was about six feet away from me. The timing couldn't have been better, and he left quickly. The worker from social services said they could put me up in a hotel for the night.

I went back to Terry again, and soon became very sick. I had such bad pains in my stomach, I was vomiting regularly. A hospital visit was a disaster as they were unable to diagnose my problem. Then Terry had to be escorted from the premises when he made a scene with the doctor who couldn't find anything wrong with me.

When the pain got so bad I could hardly get out of bed, I went to my doctor's office. My own doctor was away. The doctor filling in examined me and concluded that I had a tubal pregnancy. I nervously laughed at the idea, but stopped when he explained the risks involved with this type of pregnancy. He told me that if the tube erupted the internal bleeding could be dangerous. I needed to go directly to the hospital where they would prep me for surgery. Since we had no phone, I explained that I wouldn't be able to go to the hospital as I had to go home first. He advised against my returning home, but I had no other choice. I went home to tell Terry I had to go to the hospital. I was terrified of surgery. Terry wanted me to go to the bank for him first so he would have some money. I arrived at the hospital in the afternoon and was in surgery by eight that evening.

The next day I was heavily medicated and Terry came to visit with Janie, I couldn't even hold Janie. On the second day Terry returned to visit and insisted that I could come home and rest on the couch while I recovered. Against the hospital staff's advice I signed myself out of the hospital and returned home.

At a follow up doctor's appointment they explained that as I had had one tubal pregnancy, I was at increased risk of another one. I asked about birth control and decided on an IUD, though the doctor warned me that having had a tubal pregnancy my risks were higher than normal and an IUD would further increase the risk of another tubal pregnancy.

When I arrived home to say I had spent $30 on an IUD, I thought Terry would lose his mind. He hollered and ranted that it was a waste of money as he wouldn't touch me if I was the last person on earth. He threw chairs at me and beat me up pretty good.

I guess I should have known that being safe for the cost of a case of beer would result in this type of behaviour on Terry's part.

Some of The Outlaws motorcycle gang had been hanging around our house trying to recruit Terry. They promised to set him up with a motorcycle built for his peg leg. When bike parts started showing up in the back yard I knew this time I really had to get out.

Terry often used The Outlaws as a threat to prevent me from leaving. He would say, "I'll just let the boys know and they will be watching for you." And from the clubhouse stories I had heard, it was easy to believe that Terry was the lesser of the evils.

One time in Ottawa I had called the police to come and help me, as I waited for them in a drug store. The office who showed up was about 6'2" and a large man. He was happy to help me until he asked the name of the person involved. Once I told him Terry's name he told me, " You got in yourself, and you can get out the best way you know how." He then turned and walked out leaving me standing there in the drug store. The Ottawa police department then sent me two young skinny officers who were quite concerned that Terry had been charged on numerous occasions for assaulting an officer.

They tried to convince me that we could go and get Janie and they would be able to protect me. Once in the apartment with Janie in my arms, I knew that I didn't dare turn my back on Terry, and I had no faith that the officers could protect themselves, let alone me. Again it was just easier to stay. No one was able to help me and they couldn't understand the level of fear that I had.

I did finally convince Terry to move to Kingston with me. I think he knew that I was very close to leaving no matter what, and since I was now 16, I had options and he had fewer excuses. We moved to Kingston in the spring of 1982, just before Janie's first birthday, but things didn't change much and the fights continued.

Back in Kingston, I made contact with Jane and her co-worker Kevin. Upon seeing Jane again after such a long time all I could do was cry. Of course these were tears of joy; I missed Jane and was just so happy to see her again. Whenever I had the opportunity, I stopped to have a coffee with her. She had a calming effect; she was a good listener and never judgmental. Nor was she authoritarian, never once did she specifically tell me I must do something. Actually she was a great sounding board – there to flesh out an idea with, there to help me make my own decisions. I didn't have many opportunities to see Jane at this stage. Terry only let me out of the house to do errands and I was on a time limit. If I rode my bike very fast I could make up some time and have a short visit with Jane.

I started taking correspondence courses, so that I could receive my high school diploma. Terry did his best to sabotage my efforts, but I kept working away on them whenever I had the opportunity.

Sometimes I wasn't allowed to have stamps to mail them or all the pens would go missing. A couple of times I snuck my lessons out and mailed them when I went to the grocery store. Although I had to produce a receipt along with the change when I returned from grocery shopping, I claimed I bought a drink out of a machine so there was no receipt for that. Again I understood that I wanted a different life, but I needed to start building it slowly so that when I was finally able to leave I would be able to stand on my own two feet and have some basic skills to build on.

After moving to Kingston I left again a number of times, still unsuccessfully but for longer periods. I was able to stay away for a week at a time. Police were called a few times although I never pressed charges. It quickly became obvious how few resources a city the size of Kingston has to offer, in comparison to a city the size of Ottawa.

When I left for a few days at a time, it wasn't unusual to find blood in the stairwells when I returned. This was the result of Terry getting into fights with other people while I was gone. Another time I had left he convinced the neighbour to cut his finger off to prove how much he missed me. He held his hand on the table and claimed he wouldn't move it. Of course the neighbour didn't take him seriously and chopped off half his finger, before he realised Terry was serious.

A few months after our return to Kingston, I realized I was pregnant again, and this made me sick to my stomach. I had no idea what to do. What I did know was that if I couldn't get out with one child, the odds of getting out with two were even lower. I got a referral from my doctor for an abortion. When I told Terry about it, he went nuts on me and said, along with all the usual name calling and threats, that there was no way I was having an abortion.

Despite his threats, I kept the appointment. I even left the day before to make sure I got there. When I woke up from the anaesthetic, there were four nurses holding me down. I think the drugs had given me nightmares and I was very upset that Terry hadn't showed up for the appointment.

It was getting harder to live like this, and Janie was getting big enough that when Terry was hurting me she would wrap herself around his knees and scream, "Don't hurt my mommy."

During another of my attempts to leave, when I was 16 and Janie was one, I called my former adoptive family, the Smith's, to ask for help. They agreed to provide assistance to Janie and I, and we took the bus to South River. However, Bobby was so distraught about my coming that he had to go and stay with a friend, for as long as I was there. William and Helen were quick to find me someplace else to stay so their son could come home, which I totally understood. What I had a hard time understanding was how someone who had two parents and a happy life could remain so angry at me. I was barely a blip on the radar of his life and spent in total about four months with them. His reaction made my guilt resurface, and I was happy to agree to a different living arrangement.

I moved in with a friend of theirs and tried to return to school. However, I was struggling with the rules being imposed on me. I think this is one of the hardest parts of leaving an abusive relationship. Rules have been imposed on you for so long, you have no idea who you are or what you should be doing. Being suddenly free from an abusive relationship makes it hard to follow just about any rule. After the repression I experienced due to Terry, all I wanted to do was enjoy my freedom. It was easy to rebel against the school rules because the consequences would be less severe than living and dealing with Terry. Still dealing with too many school rules at this stage just wasn't for me. I stayed with the Smith's friends for a couple more weeks before moving to the shelter in North Bay. I stayed there until I could find an apartment for myself and my daughter.

While at the shelter another resident, who had recently been released from jail, would joke around with me. I walked into the room one day and said, "Don't talk to me goof, you're on the grease". Lucky for me he thought this was hilarious coming from a little kid of 16. This was funny I am assuming because I was using prison talk, and clearly had not spent any time in prison. The biggest insult for an inmate is to be called a 'goof' and 'you're on the grease' means you are an idiot not worthy of talking to, or about.

After moving into my own apartment with just a bed and some dishes I was very lonely. The days were long with nothing to do and it was hard to go anywhere with a baby. I stayed in the apartment about a week and then I called and left a message for Terry to say I was coming back to Kingston.

This cycle of leaving and coming back continued for a little longer. Once when I had left again for a few days and Terry had the children, he took an overdose. Some neighbours contacted me to say he was in the hospital and I went home to the children. I called the hospital and they told me that they had taken his knife away. I explained the situation, and that I was in danger if he was released too soon. I asked them to call the neighbour's number when Terry was discharged, so that I would have time to make arrangements for myself and the children. In hindsight I realize I should have left immediately. However, with no family and no support system it was difficult to find anywhere to go in the middle of the night with two sleeping children.

The next morning Terry was released at about 5 a.m. They gave him his knife back, and he showed up at the house and dragged me out to the parking lot with the knife at my throat, screaming that he was going to kill me. Someone called the police, but when they showed up I said everything was OK, as I was pretty sure Terry would kill me before they could do anything.

On another occasion a police officer was called during a domestic dispute. He arrived, found me outside, then had me sit in his car with him. He continued to sit there writing notes while Terry freaked out in front of the patrol car. I was hysterical and asked him to write his notes around the corner, but the officer was not intimidated by Terry. He finally agreed to drive off, because I wouldn't stop screaming. I knew for sure, if Terry got his hands on me when still in this rage, I was dead, and a single police officer wasn't going to be able to save me.

I was finally able to leave with Janie, but Lynn was not my child and Terry had sole custody, so she remained with him. Janie and I lived on the streets in Kingston for a while. We stayed with my mother for a couple of days, but she soon said the landlady was complaining that we used too much hot water so we couldn't stay with her any longer.

We then slept in the van of my mother's boyfriend for a few days. When he left for work at 5 a.m. he would wake us up, and I would spend the days and some nights just walking all over Kingston, carrying Janie on my shoulder. I met a lady named Beth who lived in the country, and she offered to take Janie at night and return her to me in the morning. This was helpful, because I could ride my bike around town at night and not have to carry a small child all night long.

It took me from mid-August until early November to find an apartment. I was able to rent a one bedroom apartment across the street from my mother's house. During this time I was involved with a court ordered assessment. The following letter contains psychiatric information pertaining to Terry, myself, Martha, and the children. It was done to determine the issue of Janie and Lynn's custody. Who would be the most appropriate parent? Who would best serve the children's needs?

KINGSTON GENERAL HOSPITAL
Kingston, Ontario, Canada, K7L 2V7
Telephone 613-547-2121

Department of Psychiatry,
Family Court Clinic
24 Barrie Street,

November 23, 1983.

Judge
Provincial Court (Family Division),
469 Montreal Street,
Kingston, Ontario

Re: Brenda Secor, Terry and Martha
And children Lynn d.o.b. 27/02/76
And Janie d.o.b. 6/4/81

Dear Judge:

The above named parties were referred to the family court clinic for assessment in a custody and access matter. Terry and Martha are the parents of Lynn, 7 years old. Terry and Brenda are the parents of Janie, 2 years old. Lynn presently resides with Terry and Janie with Brenda. Martha has made application for custody of Lynn and Terry has applied for custody of Janie.

In order to complete a meaningful assessment for the court, the following interviews were conducted: Terry was seen individually on October 6th, 18th and November 8th and 21st; he attended the Clinic with his daughter Lynn on October 26th; I met with Mr. Hilton Murray in regards to Terry on October 28th; Brenda attended the Clinic with her daughter Janie on October

17th and 24th, and November 17th. I met with Jane, Children's Aid Society worker, in regards to Brenda on November 18th; Martha was seen with her husband on October 7th, individually on November 4th and with Lynn on November 22nd.

Background Information:

Terry and Martha married when Martha was pregnant with Lynn. Both report early dissatisfaction with the marriage. Martha alleges that Terry was physically abusive towards her, particularly when drinking. She states that she was extremely fearful of Terry. In Martha's account, she and Terry were together until Lynn was approximately 2 1/2 years old. She states that she left Lynn with Terry only out of fear as he had threatened recrimination were she to attempt to take the child with her. Martha reports that she has always maintained contact with the Children's Aid Society to ensure that Lynn's well-being was monitored. She adds that she did make efforts to maintain contact with Lynn but, for fear for herself and for Lynn needed to submit to Terry's dictates around visiting. In her account, Terry did finally allow her to begin weekly visits with Lynn prior to their divorce. She visited with Lynn each Friday for some period of time. In Martha's account, visits ceased at the time of her divorce from Terry when he moved and gave her no knowledge of his whereabouts. According to Martha, Terry has called her on a number of occasions up until quite recently *offering her custody of Lynn and then again ceasing contact and not following through on plans made. Terry's account contrasts to that given by Martha. According to him, he and Martha separated when Lynn was 1 year old and Martha failed to make any effort to keep in contact with Lynn for several years following. In his view, only at the time of their divorce approximately two years ago did Martha show any interest in visiting rights. She visited with Lynn once weekly for a period following that. He adds that he did not see Martha being very interested in time with Lynn when she did visit. Terry does admit that he was fairly abusive towards Martha. He does not agree, however, that his violence and Martha's fear militated against her taking Lynn with her. Rather, he maintains that Martha had minimal interest in the child. Terry does state that after his move from Ottawa to Kingston, he put a stop to Martha's access to Lynn for some period of time. He attributes his action to Brenda's alleged displeasure around Martha's visit to their home.*

Brenda and Terry cohabited for approximately 2 1/2 years preceding their recent separation. Brenda was 14 years old when she began living with Terry. Terry is 16 years her senior. Brenda feels, in retrospect, that Terry's offers of caring and company overshadowed her better judgment to his abusiveness towards her. Terry agrees that he was physically violent with Brenda. He states that the separation was his fault, that due to alcohol abuse and violent behavior towards Brenda. Terry states that he is aware that

Brenda had no choice but to leave him. Initially, Brenda left Terry with taking both children with her, but has since returned Lynn to Terry. When this case was first referred to the Court Clinic, Brenda had applied for custody of both Lynn and Janie but has since altered that and is now seeking custody of only Janie.

Terry:

Terry presents as a somewhat disheveled looking gentleman. He has one wooden leg and hands covered in tattoos. Terry describes a turbulent childhood and adolescence. He is the eldest of four siblings. In his view, his mother always disliked him that evidenced in early years by her abusiveness towards him. Terry recalls frequent runaway incidents beginning at age 11 or 12. One of these incidents resulted in Terry losing one foot when he was attempting to jump onto a moving train. A series of institutional placements began when Terry was 14 and sent to training school. That was followed by a number of imprisonments for a variety of charges including drug offences, robbery, and breaking and entering. Terry states that he was last in prison in 1975. He has been charged with several offences since that time, those resulting in fines or probation terms.

In the course of assessment, Terry has tended to alternate between self-denigration and outward projection of blame for the difficulties which he encounters. He described himself as depressed. He conveys an overall sense of dissatisfaction with the course his life has taken thus far and, at the same time a great deal of pessimism around his ability to alter events or his own feelings. Terry shares his discomfort with a notion of changing his "image", referring to his manner of dress and general demeanour. He appears to feel that those around him expect a certain type of deportment and would see himself as needing to start afresh in a new location among new people in order to make any changes. In reference to his violent behavior, Terry states that he has always had problems in relating to women. In his report, he attended one counseling session sometime ago. The counselor apparently asked Terry to write down the occasions that he had hit women. Terry did not wish to and attended no further counseling sessions. Terry attributes his difficulties with women at least in part to his relationship with his mother but, again, conveys little hope for change in that regard. While on the one hand seeming to blame himself for problematic behaviours and situations, Terry presents as a gentleman who sees himself as victimized by the courts and the "system" in general. Terry has said several times that he felt he was being treated badly by the courts. In addition, he has had some difficulty in reaching out to community resources in times of need as he feels that he is not liked and received well at places such as the Children's Aid Society.

Terry's abuse of alcohol stands out as a notable problem. From his own descriptions, excessive alcohol use would seem to be a chronic and long standing problem. I asked Terry whether he would consider an antabuse program. He responded that he did not see himself as able to give up his drinking particularly when he is feeling depressed. He clearly did convey the sense that he looks to alcohol as a way to deal with and, perhaps, dull unpleasant or unhappy feelings. In Terry's report, he does not see his alcohol use as impacting negatively on his care of either child.

In discussions with Terry about his daughters, I have found him largely focused on his own needs rather than theirs. He is a gentleman who sees himself as having little that is positive in his life and appears to look to the girls for some heightened sense of self-esteem. Terry says quite clearly that, without Lynn, he would have nothing and be nothing. Several times in the course of assessment Terry has indicated that he may not pursue custody of Janie. He attributes that not to Janie's interests but, rather to his own upset around difficulties he has experienced in securing access to his younger daughter. He conveys the message that if others persist in making things difficult for him he might just as well give up the battle for Janie. Similarly, in a November 8th interview, Terry said that he might well call Martha and tell her to come and get Lynn. He related that to his sense that, in some manner, the system would conspire against him to ensure that his *daughter is taken from him. Were he to lose Lynn, he envisions a very sad state of affairs. In his words, "Lynn is all I've got, if I lost her, I wouldn't last long".*

Terry does convey a sincere caring for both Janie and Lynn. Unfortunately, he sees himself having very little control over events and, in his preoccupation with the difficulties he has been encountering; he appears to lose sight of what might be in the children's best interests.

<u>*Brenda Secor:*</u>

Brenda is the 18 year old mother of Janie. Brenda recounts a turbulent childhood and adolescence. She spent her early years with an alcoholic mother who, in her description was neglectful and abusive towards her. Brenda describes an earlier decision not again to place herself in this type of situation in which she was with her mother. Despite that, she recounts finding herself in just such a situation with Terry where, by his own admission, he drank excessively and was abusive towards her. Brenda certainly does appear to have some understanding of the dynamics in her relationship with Terry; at a time when she was feeling much need for somebody to care about her and provide companionship.

Brenda presents as a fairly bright, verbally adept young woman. She has experienced a number of difficulties in her life. Quite recently, Brenda was without a place of residence and her arrangements had been somewhat make shift. She had arranged for Janie to spend her nights with a friend until she was able to find suitable accommodation. Brenda did procure an apartment as of November 1st and she and Janie are now residing there together. Brenda speaks of her wishes to engage in a more productive course of action. She states, for example that she would like to enroll in an upgrading program. However, she appears at this point in time to stop short of pursuing her goals. Brenda finds her present circumstances somewhat depressing. She has few financial resources to make her apartment a more home-like surrounding. Brenda states that she finds herself sleeping a great deal of late as a way of coping with depressed feelings. Brenda strikes me as a young woman with low self-esteem. Difficulties she has encountered thus far have left her somewhat untrusting of those around her. Brenda describes the difficulties she has going into new situations or dealing with strangers. She has nonetheless, maintained several long term and supportive relationships with several people, those including a Worker from Sunnyside Children's Centre and Jane from the Children's Aid Society. In addition, Brenda has attended some counseling sessions with a counselor at Sunnyside Children's Centre. Brenda speaks warmly of another woman who had worked with the Children's Aid Society and has since returned to continue her schooling. Brenda has looked to this woman, as well, for supports in times of need.

Martha:

Martha, as detailed above, recounts an early history of extreme turbulence in her marriage to Terry. Since their separation, Martha has remarried. She expresses satisfaction with her marriage and describes her present living situation as stable.

Martha is the mother to Lynn, 7 years old. Martha has made application for custody of her daughter Lynn. In her account her application for custody was motivated by knowledge of Brenda leaving Terry. Martha felt that, with a woman in the house to assist in Lynn's caretaking, Lynn probably should not be removed from her father with whom she has resided consistently since birth. As detailed earlier, Martha states that she left Lynn with her father out of fear for recrimination by Terry against herself.

Martha has presented as fairly anxious throughout assessment. On a number of occasions she expressed concern about Terry being privy to the information which she was sharing with me. Martha states that she continues to fear that Terry will be violent either towards her or members of her family if her actions or statements anger him. That notwithstanding, Martha has expressed her intention to proceed with her custody application feeling that she cannot continue to determine her actions in response to the degree of intimidation which she feels that Terry is exerting. Primarily, Martha has express worry about Terry's ability to care for Lynn as a single parent. She points to his *excessive drinking as militating against his parental adequacy. In addition, Martha wonders about the possible detriment to Lynn of being exposed to a number of mothering figures. In her account, following her separation from Terry he was involved with a young woman for a period of time that followed by his cohabitation with Brenda. Martha does express awareness that Lynn was fond of and close to Brenda and then to her sister Janie.*

In the course of assessment, Martha has presented with some ambivalence and confusion in regards to her custody application. As pointed out earlier, she reports continuing fear of Terry and wonders were Lynn with her, would she be placing herself and family members in danger. In addition, she continues to question whether it would, in fact, be in Lynn's best interest to be removed from her father with whom she has consistently resided.

During the assessment period, Martha has taken advantage of whatever opportunities Terry has offered her to spend time with Lynn. Despite the travelling distance from her home outside Ottawa, Ontario, she has been willing to travel to Kingston at anytime that she felt that she might be able to see Lynn.

Martha's husband attended one interview with his wife. He presents as a quiet perhaps somewhat passive gentleman. He expressed an openness to have Lynn reside in his home. Further, he appeared sincere in sharing the enjoyment he derived from time spent with Lynn in the past.

The Children:

Janie: Janie is an active, verbal and personable young child of 2 years old. She is a bright little girl who would appear to be developing well and in an age appropriate manner. She appeared to have little difficulty in relating to her surroundings or to myself in the course of assessment interviews. Janie is full of enthusiasm and eagerness in her play.

Lynn: Lynn is an attractive and, again, very personable child. In some respects, she appeared to me advanced for her 7 years. She presented as extremely verbally adept. Lynn has a good command of letters and words and her writing and drawing abilities are impressive.

Lynn suffers from cystic fibrosis and requires ongoing monitoring, medication and physical therapy several times daily.

Lynn has, clearly, experienced some degree of instability and turbulence in her 7 years. Her father has proven her only consistent caretaker during that period of time. In our first interview, Lynn shared her discomfort in attending a new school and meeting new children, that seemingly related to the reactions that strangers have to her illness.

Present Situation:

I would like to move on now to consideration of the questions of custody and access in this matter. I would like to look first at those issues in relation to Janie, 2 years old.

Janie is presently residing with her mother, Brenda. As detailed earlier, Brenda is a young woman who experienced a turbulent childhood and adolescence and continues to report some difficulties in the areas of day-to-day management and in relationships with others. By her own report, Brenda's mother abused alcohol and was neglectful and abusive towards her. Brenda was a ward of the Children's Aid Society from approximately age 8 until her 18th birthday in November of this year. Brenda was 14 when she began residing with Terry.

Brenda appears to enjoy a warm and affectionate relationship with her daughter, Janie. Certainly, one would expect that the individual difficulties which Brenda continues to experience will have some impact in parenting areas. Brenda does, however, appear to work hard to ensure that Janie is properly nurtured and cared for. When they were without adequate lodging, she ensured that Janie had a suitable place to spend her overnights. She was attentive not only to the physical surroundings but, in addition, was attentive to the quality of the relationship between Janie and the woman who was assisting in her caretaking. Jane, who has been involved with Brenda since she was 8 years old and became a ward of the Children's Aid Society, agreed that Brenda continues to have some personal difficulties. She felt, however, that were those difficulties to impact on Janie, that Brenda would not hesitate to enlist the assistance of the resources available to her. In looking at the custody issue, this stands out as a key area to address. Terry, in contrast to Brenda, appears fairly closed to the use of outside resources. In the context of assessment, Terry has presented as a gentleman who, in reaction to difficulties and stress, becomes depressed and confused as opposed to action oriented. In his view of himself as victimized by the system, he appears to discount the potential usefulness of community resources. It concerns me, further, that Terry appears to have little notion of the potential impact of his excessive drinking on his parenting abilities. On a practical level, in a first interview with Terry, he did state that his minimal financial resources and the difficulties there inherent were due at least in part to his excessive spending on alcohol. Mr. Murray with whom I discussed Terry expressed some clear concerns about the impact of this gentleman's drinking on his functioning as a parent. In Mr. Murray's view, when Terry is drinking, that activity takes priority over the needs of those around him. Mr. Murray proffers the view that Terry looks to his children to meet his own needs rather than examining the manner in which he might meet theirs. Mr. Murray goes on to say that in approximately two years that he has been involved with Terry, Terry has not at any time shown that he could maintain sobriety for any reasonable length of time. Further, he has found Terry closed to the notion of an antabuse program to deal with his abuse of alcohol.

I feel that Terry's expression of caring for his children is certainly sincere. It is my feeling, further, that the practical and emotional problems which he experiences certainly have the potential to impact on his parenting abilities. Terry discounts both his own ability to alter his circumstances and the potential helpfulness of outside resources. I recommend at this time that Janie remain in the custody of her mother, Brenda. Despite the difficulties which she has encountered and continues to encounter, Brenda displays an ability and willingness for self examination. Further, she has maintained several long-standing and supportive relationships in the community and I feel that, were Janie's well being endangered in any way, Brenda would look for assistance for her daughter.

I would like to move on now to the custody issue in relation to Lynn. I have dealt in some detail throughout this report with concerns which emerge in looking at Terry. As stated above, I see problem areas in his own functioning as certainly having the potential to impact on his adequacy as a parent. In terms of looking at Lynn's needs, Terry makes blanket statements about his ability to care for her. He views any threat to his custody of Lynn as an element of the manner in which he is victimized by others. Mr. Murray expresses concern that, in the absence of a woman in his life, Terry might, particularly as Lynn gets older, transfer his inappropriate reactions to women onto Lynn.

I met with Lynn on two occasions. At both times, she expressed a desire to remain with her father. On the first occasion that I saw her, Lynn said that she would not like to see her mother even in the context of an office interview. Her attitude in that regard had changed considerably by the second time that I saw her. Between our first and second interview, Terry had made arrangements for Lynn to spend a week with Martha. He stated to myself on the day that Lynn was leaving that she was excited about her visit. I saw Lynn with Martha on the day that she was to return home to her father. At that time, she was extremely playful and affectionate with her mother. When seen on the first occasion, Lynn had referred to her mother as Martha. When seen with Martha, she appeared quite natural in calling her mommy. I saw Lynn alone for the latter portion of the interview. At that time, she said that she still wished to remain with her father but would want to see her mother on some weekends. She added "not every weekend". I would want to add that I was impressed by the quality of interaction between Martha and Lynn when they were seen together. There was a warm and natural affection between them. Both spoke with a great deal of pleasure about the time that they had spent together over the previous week. Lynn seemed, as well, to have derived pleasure out of contacts with her mother's extended family. She said she had missed her father and her sister Janie.

As this report illustrates, I have serious concerns about Terry's ongoing ability to address both the practical and emotional needs that his daughter Lynn has. Most recently, Terry expressed worry about an assault charge that he is presently facing and possible imprisonment if he is found guilty. In regards to how he would ensure Lynn's caretaking were he in fact imprisoned I have had varying responses from Terry. On one occasion he stated that he would have to leave this area because he could not go to prison; were that to occur, he could not take Lynn with him because he would be found more easily. On another occasion he said that he would have Martha care for Lynn if he were in prison. On a third occasion he said he did not know what he would do. In terms of his place of residence, when seen for a first interview in October, Terry informed me that he had been recently evicted from an apartment on Parkway Street and that he and Lynn were residing with friends. He further stated that the situation was not the best for Lynn because there were dogs in the house where they were residing and that, given that Lynn has cystic fibrosis, the dogs were a potential health hazard for his daughter. Terry was unable to secure an alternate residence due to financial difficulties. As far as I am aware, he has not yet relocated.

As indicated earlier, Martha has expressed some confusion and ambivalence in relation to her custody application for Lynn. She continues to express ambivalence in that regard. Martha states that contacts which she has with Terry only add to her confusion. She continues to worry about the actions he might take towards herself and her family were she given custody of Lynn. Martha asked me if I would share my recommendation with her to assist her in deciding whether she should pursue her custody application. I expressed concern to Martha about her looking to my recommendation as part of her decision-making.

Given a lack of clarity about Martha's position in this matter, I find myself unable to make a firm custody recommendation in regards to Lynn. I have outlined above a number of very serious concerns about Terry and his functioning. Were Lynn to remain with him, I would suggest that the Children's Aid Society be enlisted to monitor that situation.

I understand that access has been problematic for all parties in this matter. At the present time, Terry and Brenda have been dealing with the Family referral and conciliation services in making access arrangements. I would see it most useful for them to continue to use that service in regards to access. I would see any access arrangements considered so that Janie and Lynn have ongoing contact with each other. It is difficult to be more specific in regards to access until a decision is made about Lynn's place of residence.

Hoping that this report is useful to Your Honour, I remain,

Yours truly,

Family Court Clinic

Fortunately for Janie and me this report gave me more credibility as a parent than it did Terry. For years Terry had tried to brainwash me into thinking he was the better parent. But this report conclusively indicates otherwise. The clinician has shown that Terry is an emotional basket case. His suitability as a parent is clearly drawn into question. How could he cope with two children on a daily basis when the clinician has deep reservations about Terry's ability to look after just one – his first daughter Lynn.

The court in view of the foregoing psychiatric assessment, had some respect for my position and agreed to allow us to make the transfers of Janie through the court house on Montreal St. I would drop her off, then leave. Terry would arrive, pick Janie up for the weekend, and return her to the court office on Sunday. He would then leave. I would arrive and retrieve Janie.

This only worked for the first couple of visits before all hell broke loose, again. One day Terry decided to wait for us in the bushes outside the courthouse. As Janie and I passed, he quickly emerged from cover and in a blink Janie was in his arms. "I just want to carry her for you," he would say in a proud yet threatening manner. As if he was doing me some sort of favour, I would think. Again, I was powerless to do much. Physically, I couldn't take Janie from him, so he walked with me to my apartment. At the apartment I tried to call my mother, to ask her to call the police. I figured I could make this a quick phone call and not get caught, but the phone line was busy and I couldn't get through. By then Terry had come in and made himself at home.

It took me weeks to get him out. In the end I resorted to calling Children's Aid and having Kevin have a chat with him. Kevin worked with Jane and had known me for many years. During this extended visit the fighting and abuse resumed. I didn't have any way to get him out of my apartment. Fear is the main reason I didn't involve the police. But once, when he started making threats, I picked up a big knife and to my astonishment he ran. I laughed so hard, as I remembered he had always said it would be a cold day in hell before he ran from me.

Janie is the reason I was able to make changes in my life. Although I had said "never me" while growing up in an environment of physical abuse, I had stayed in an abusive relationship. This was almost certainly because my own childhood made me believe it was normal, even though I had dreams of escaping.

I watched Janie growing daily and couldn't help but feel I was setting her up to repeat the pattern. I thought long and hard about how I would feel if she were to end up in a similar situation. I thought long and hard about what was in Janie's best interests and was determined to provide her with a life that would break the pattern.

It was clear to me she needed me and that I had to provide her with the tools she needed to build a better life. It took me longer to realize that I needed her as much, if not more, than she needed me. Together we were a team, and we could face the world together.

There is no doubt in my mind that without her, I wouldn't have made it to my twenties. My self-destructive behaviour, and my life-threatening relationships would have killed me. I had taken overdoses as a child and a few while living with Terry. I was pretty sure the only way to get away from Terry would be to die. If I didn't do it, it was just a matter of time until he did.

The toolkit I was building for Janie started with role modeling. I had to show her a different life, so that she could, with my help, build a better life for herself. She was my reason for getting up each morning. In some ways I was lucky not knowing how hard this was going to be. The difficulties I would face were clearly unknown to me. Still, when they did occur, I knew beyond doubt that I had to overcome them and provide Janie with a much better life than the one I experienced as a child. One where she would have the opportunity to reach her fullest potential.

NEW BEGINNINGS
18-25 years of age

After all my attempts, I finally left Terry for good in the spring of 1984, just prior to Janie's third birthday. There had been a big fight at a friend's house, which went on for hours. I was only able to leave by climbing down the balcony. I returned shortly after to pick up Janie. Terry was again camped out in my apartment and I used threats of police in order to be able to leave with Janie. I had reached my limits, tired of responding in fear. The worst he could do was hit me, and I didn't care. I was taking Janie with me whether he liked it or not.

Following this big fight I slept for about 22 hours. When I woke up I began thinking about how I could start making new friends; who might I call, that sort of thing. Part of the difficulty of staying away from Terry was the loneliness and isolation. Not having any friends made it difficult, but I was going to give it my best shot this time as I knew that Janie needed a better, more stable environment.

One person who came to mind was an old neighbour, Anthony. I decided to give him a call to see if he would like to go for coffee. The only problem was I didn't have any contact information for him. He used to live with a lady named Lisa next door to us, but I was aware they had gone their separate ways. I decided to call Lisa to see if she had a phone number for Anthony. I called pretending I was looking for his friend. She may have seen through this, but she gave me his phone number anyway. I gave Anthony a call, we met for coffee at the corner of Princess and Division; and the rest, as they say, is history.

Anthony and I started dating in April of 1984. He would take Janie and I out for pizza and on trips to Brockville to have lunch at a deli he liked. By July 1984 Anthony and I moved in together. I was worried about how Janie would handle this, I didn't want to be moving anyone in and out of her life. Janie and I talked and I explained that Anthony was going to live with us for a while. I made sure not to promise forever. I didn't want to make a promise that I couldn't keep.

We rented an apartment and I got my first job, providing in-home assistance to the elderly. Adjusting to my new relationship took some time. I wasn't used to being allowed to go out and having no one timing my absence. It seemed too good to be true and it was a long time before I stopped waiting for the other shoe to drop.

Terry was still a part of my life. He was either trying to convince me to meet him or trying to convince me that Anthony was a bad guy. What kept me from going back to Terry was Anthony and the fear that if I returned to Terry, he wouldn't be there waiting for me when I came back. Anthony was what I had been looking for – he even passed the checklist I had created for my next relationship. With Jane's help I came up with a list of important qualities for my next relationship.

The list included things such as:

- must have a job
- must not be an alcoholic
- must not have been in prison
- must not be controlling or abusive
- must not have children

This list was very basic and was based entirely on my experiences with Terry. Unfortunately, selfish as it may seem, I knew I would be bringing my own baggage into a new relationship, but I was in no position to accommodate someone else's baggage. And, I don't mean to take this out on another person's children, but my experience with a step child had been very negative. Lynn, Terry's daughter from a previous marriage, had been turned into a psychological weapon. It hurt both me and Lynn and I knew I could never do that again. The inclusion of a step child also makes leaving a relationship very difficult because you are also abandoning that child. I found leaving Lynn behind one of the most difficult parts about leaving Terry. I didn't want any part of hurting another child. It was therefore very important that my next partner did not have any children for me to worry about.

Not only did Anthony pass my checklist, he went beyond my expectations, and encouraged me to do things like continue my education, get a driver's license, and my first job. Although I was doing so much more, we still had time to take Janie to the park and play with her. And things were much calmer for Janie; she was living a normal life.

Jane continued to be an important part of my new life by offering support and encouragement. She would be the most important person in my life for many years to come, and it was a blessing that Anthony totally understood this. Jane could pull the positives out of any situation and she continued to believe that I could do anything I set my mind to. Anthony also supported and believed in me and the support of these two people enabled me to keep moving forward, one step at a time. My small goals, with their encouragement, were reached. In doing so I was able to set bigger goals that also became attainable.

For the first time in my life I had people I could count on. Jane and Anthony were my shelter in the middle of the tornado. Their support was so important, that I couldn't imagine disappointing either one of them. I never took this support system for granted, as I knew first-hand what it was like to have no support of any kind.

During the early years of our relationship I never thought about Anthony leaving or about how long it would last. I viewed each day as a gift, a new start. I started taking correspondence courses to complete my high school diploma. Anthony helped around the house, and although I didn't realize he could cook for the first year, he did a lot of dishes. For our first anniversary he made me a teriyaki steak dinner and I was delighted and surprised to learn he could cook. Our first Christmas together he bought me all kinds of presents, a new coat, new pyjamas and many other items. I was very surprised as these were the first gifts I had received from anyone other than Jane since I lived in foster care. I was like a little kid opening all those presents.

I am not going to say we didn't have disagreements; however, a disagreement was just that, no hidden agendas. It took time to adjust to a life without abuse. I suffered from post-traumatic stress syndrome, and was often jumpy, especially when startled. I think Anthony felt bad as he was usually the one who startled me. It wasn't him. It was the result of years of looking over my shoulder and never knowing what to expect.

I often had bad nightmares and would wake up screaming at the top of my lungs. I am sure on a few occasions I woke the neighbours as well as my family. But these nightmares about Terry were allowing me to move forward.

Janie was having visits with Terry, and although I found this stressful for both her and me, I thought it was important that she knew who her real father was. I knew what it was like to have no father. We tried to make the access work, but in a short period of time Terry had a new relationship and was beating up his new girlfriend during Janie's visits. I had serious issues with this. I had worked hard to get her out of the violent setting and here I was being forced to send her back every other weekend to endure the violence again on her own.

As Anthony and I celebrated our second year together by moving into a new apartment, Terry started to show up again. Sometimes when I left the apartment I would see him walking down the other side of the street. We had gone back to court, and I had asked for a no access order as he was beating up his new girlfriend when Janie was there. When I would be packing Janie's bag for a weekend with Terry, she would be unpacking it saying she didn't want to go. I tried to explain that the courts said she had to go but this doesn't mean much to a four year old.

I also tried to explain to Terry, somewhat inappropriately I might add, that he had 26 days per month to beat up his girlfriend but that for the 4 days Janie was with him he could use some restraint. My concern however was only for Janie, and not for Terry's unfortunate new girlfriend. In his twisted way of thinking, Terry tried to justify abusing his girlfriend in Janie's presence by claiming, "he was just teaching Janie the facts of life." This statement is what caused me to go for the no access order. I was trying to create a different life for Janie and it did not include her witnessing anyone getting beat up.

I contacted my lawyer and requested that we try for a no access order. He didn't think it would be successful, but he agreed to start the process.

What follows is another court ordered psychiatric assessment. It too would be forwarded to the family court judge. It was my hope the judge would see how skewed Terry's thinking was. How psychopathically ill he must be to claim that beating up his new girlfriend in Janie's presence was teaching her 'the facts of life'.

KINGSTON GENERAL HOSPITAL
Kingston, Ontario, Canada, K7L 2V7
Telephone 613-547-2121

Department of Psychiatry
Family Court Clinic
24 Barrie Street

March 23, 1988.

Judge
Provincial Court (Family Division),
469 Montreal Street,
Kingston, Ontario

Re: Brenda Secor, Terry and child Janie d.o.b 6/4/81

Dear Judge:

Brenda and Terry were referred to the Family Court Clinic for assessment and report in an access matter. Brenda and Terry are the parents of Janie, six years eleven months old. They have not resided together since 1984. Janie has lived with her mother throughout. Terry has exercised access, seemingly somewhat intermittently as he has been fairly mobile. Brenda curtailed Terry's access to Janie in March 1987, and he has not seen the child since that time.

This matter was referred to the Court Clinic in October 1987. Appointments with Brenda, Janie and Brenda's partner Anthony progressed smoothly. Brenda was seen individually on October 27th, 1987 and January 22, 1988. Brenda, her partner, *and Janie attended on November 6, 1987. Janie was seen individually on November 13, 1987. There was a considerable delay in seeing Terry. Release conditions imposed on him pending disposition of a criminal charge prevented Terry from leaving Hastings County to attend appointments. His attorney was able to have that condition changed, and Terry and his wife Paula were interviewed on December 22, 1987. Terry attended for psychological testing on January 12, 1988, (The report of that testing is addenda to this report). Efforts later in January and into February to contact Terry and his wife, both by phone and letter, to arrange additional appointments proved fruitless. Terry's lawyer has since informed me that his client was incarcerated pending disposition of new criminal charges. Terry was very recently sentenced to five and a half months in jail for two assault charges and two charges of breach of probation. As I will be commencing a six month leave of absence on April 8th, I felt that it would be useful to the court if I communicated around those areas where I have been able to draw conclusions. As I will detail, I am not able, at this point, to recommend around whether access with her father is in Janie's best interest. To do so would require additional individual interview time with Terry and interviews with father and daughter. I believe that Janie wishes to see her father, while conveying upset with what she describes as her father's drinking and assaultive behavior towards his wife which*

Janie states she has witnessed. Janie expressed distress with some of Paula's verbal treatment of her.

I will outline my concerns about the potential impact on Janie, over the long term, of exposure to her father's controlling and abusive manner with female partners, and concerns about stability, predictability, and role modeling in the context of access visits.

The parties to the present dispute were assessed at the Court Clinic in 1983 in a custody matter. Terry and Brenda were disputing custody of Janie. Martha, mother of Terry's older daughter Lynn, had applied for custody of that child. Lynn had been living with her father since her parent's separation. I understand that she has since taken up residence with her mother in Ottawa. Although I have had limited contact with Terry in the context of the present assessment, my previous involvement afforded me considerable background information.

Terry:

In a 1983 assessment, Terry indicated that he was the eldest of four siblings. He described a turbulent childhood and adolescence. He felt that his mother always disliked him, evident in early years by her abusiveness towards him. Terry spoke of frequent run away incidents, beginning at age eleven or twelve.

One of those episodes resulted in Terry losing a foot when he attempted to jump onto a moving train. A series of institutional placements began, Terry said, when he was fourteen and sent to Training School. That was followed by a number of incarcerations for a variety of charges including drug offences, robbery, and breaking and entering. In the context of the 1983 assessment, Terry states that he was last in jail in 1975. He had, he said been charged with several offences after 1975, these resulting in fines or probation terms.

In the earlier assessment, Terry tended to alternate between self-denigration and outward projection of blame for difficulties. He conveyed an overall sense of dissatisfaction with the course his life had taken to that point, and a great deal of pessimism around his ability to alter events. He presented as a gentleman who saw himself as victimized by the courts and the "system" in general. In the 1983 assessment, in matters related to his children, I saw Terry as very focused on his own needs. He spoke of Lynn in terms of the impact on himself were he to lose her. He expressed ambivalence about pursuing custody of Janie, again related to the impact on himself.

Terry described, in the earlier assessment, chronic difficulties in relating to women. He admitted to being physically abusive of both Martha and Brenda and, again, conveyed pessimism with his ability to change. Terry has tended to choose very young women as partners. Brenda was only 14 when she began a relationship with Terry, is 16 years his junior. Paula, Terry's wife, was a teenager of approximately 18, when they formed their union, she is 18 years his junior. Paula, like Martha and Brenda, has been assaulted by Terry. In the context of a previous assessment, both Martha and Brenda described feeling very fearful of and intimidated by Terry. Brenda both then and now, saw him as controlling and intimidating both physically and psychologically. In only one interview with Terry and Paula, I sensed an element of Terry's control in descriptions of the couple's dealings as parents. Terry and Paula spoke of fairly serious disagreements about child rearing, with Terry seeming to take a directive approach that assumed that he was right and Paula was wrong.

Alcohol abuse has been a chronic problem for Terry. During a 1983 assessment, Terry did not envision giving up drinking and, further, did not believe that his drinking impacted negatively on his parenting. My impression, in an interview on December 22, 1987, was that Terry had continued to experience significant problems with alcohol abuse. In 1987, a two year probation term resulted from assault and weapons charges, and Terry was required to attend an alcohol rehabilitation program, as well as a group for assaultive men. A September 1987 assessment at the Belleville A.T.A.C. Centre indicated "substantial alcohol and drug dependence, requiring structured treatment. In our December interview, Terry reported very positive results from the programs he was attending, stating that he'd had one "slip" in drinking in the previous 10 weeks. A January 12, 1988 report from Serenity House where Terry was attending a treatment program for alcohol and drug dependency indicated that Terry was admitted to the day treatment program on October 5 1987, and, at his own request, recommitted himself on December 7, 1987. The report described very positive participation in the program on Terry's part since recommitment in December. "He is now highly motivated, eager to learn, and seems genuinely pleased to attend the daily group sessions. Terry has gained confidence, self-respect, and portrays a positive self-image. Since December 7, 1987, Terry has complied with all obligations of his program in a very willing and responsible manner". There is no commentary in the report on the nature of Terry's participation prior to December 7th.

As in the past, when interviewed in December, I noted Terry's tendency to project blame outward for difficulties. Specifically, he attributed an assault on Paula, for which he was charged in April, 1987, to difficulties with access to Janie, and to Brenda purportedly making things difficult for him. Unfortunately, Paula appeared to endorse Terry's projection and failure to take responsibility for his abusive treatment of her by making excuses for Terry's behavior and taking blame upon herself. She said, "I guess I came onto him", arguing about little things and being moody while pregnant with the couple's child.

Although Terry, when seen in December, reported positive results from programs for alcohol abuse and for assaultive behavior, and staff of those programs spoke well of his participation, recent charges speak to continuation of chronic patterns. Terry was recently convicted for two charges of assault, and two of breach of probation. These charges, apparently, arise again from assaults on his wife, Paula and in his lawyer's report, are alcohol-related. Terry's lawyer informed me, as well, that Paula describes the marriage as over, asserting that she is not open to reconciliation.

I have had strong concerns, in considering Janie's access to her father, about her visiting in her father's home where she would potentially be witness to Terry being abusive towards his wife. This is concerning in terms of the initial upset to which Janie has attested as well as the impact over time on the way that Janie sees herself in the context of relationships with men. Girls exposed to those sorts of abusive situations are more likely to place themselves in relationships, as adults, where they are victims. They are often left with a sense of "Lacking control and power in their own lives. With changed circumstances – i.e., the Terry and Paula's separation – one does not know at this point what Terry's living situation will be on release from jail. Were he and Paula to reconcile, Janie's continued exposure to that situation would be a concern. Given Terry's pattern of abusiveness towards female partners, that concern would need to be addressed, as well, in the context of future relationships into which her father might enter. Terry's drinking, as well, poses a major concern in regards to access. Janie has reported regular drinking on her father's part during access visits.

Over the long term, one would need to be concerned about the projection of Terry's difficulties with women onto Janie. Terry has formed controlling, abusive relationships with very young women. One has to question his ability, when Janie reached adolescence, to tolerate moves towards independence and individuation on her part. Even at this point Janie, in envisioning a joint meeting at the Clinic with her father, was quite anxious. She did not appear to feel that she could express herself openly with her father.

Brenda Secor:

Brenda was a young mother of eighteen when first assessed in 1983. In her childhood, Brenda was in a deprived family situation. In Brenda's description, her mother was an alcoholic *who was neglectful and abusive towards her. At fourteen, at a time when she was feeling much need for someone to be caring towards her, Brenda saw Terry as able to provide caring and companionship.*

When seen in 1983, Brenda presented as quite a bright, insightful young woman who was open to self-examination. Although she was experiencing some practical difficulties in her own functioning, and seemed somewhat depressed, she emerged as child focused, ensuring Janie's well being at all times. Brenda maintained long-term, positive relationships with several helping professionals in the community, this offering supports for herself and Janie.

Seeing Brenda four years later, she appears to have used her potential positively. She attends St. Lawrence college fulltime. Brenda and Janie have lived with Anthony since July, 1984. Anthony seems a gentle, unassuming young man who, in Brenda's description, is neither controlling nor abusive. As she had wanted to do even as a teenager, Brenda appears to have broken a pattern of keeping herself in abusive situations. This is positive not only for her, but in terms of the role modeling she provides for Janie. As an infant and toddler, Janie was exposed to a dysfunctional parental relationship, and to her father's abuse of her mother. In Brenda's account, when Terry was violent with her, Janie would hold his knees and cry, telling him not to hurt her mommy.

Brenda relates that she and Terry reconciled for 5 to 6 months from approximately November 1983 to April 1984. After what she describes as an abusive and humiliating incident at a friend's home, Brenda states that she refused to go home with Terry. He would not; she states let her have Janie until she threatened to involve the police. Following that, Brenda reports, Terry went to Ottawa for six months and did not initiate any access to Janie. Terry was, in Brenda's account, entitled to alternate weekends and Tuesdays. On his return from Ottawa, he exercised some access. Brenda states that, for the most part, this would only be on the Tuesdays because Terry was living at the Harbour Light, a residential treatment facility run by The Salvation Army. If Janie went for a weekend, Brenda states, the child would be upset because she had to share a bed with her father. Terry eventually got an extra mattress, and Janie was content with that. Janie, Brenda states, liked Paula from the outset of her relationship with Terry. She didn't like fights between Terry and Paula or Terry hitting Paula. Brenda was concerned that Janie, again, was exposed to a chaotic life style, characterized by drinking, fighting, and violence. As well, Janie was purportedly telling her mother that Paula was hitting her three year old son, Jason. Brenda's impression was that Janie was not allowed to talk about Anthony at her father's home. Brenda describes Janie having a particularly difficult March break visit at her father's home last year.

In her account, Janie was very upset with Paula's treatment of her, saying that Paula was verbally harsh and also denigrating Janie's mother to the child. After that, Brenda maintains, Janie said that she did not want to go to her father's if Paula was there. Shortly thereafter, Terry was incarcerated after being charged with assaulting Paula. Brenda states that he did not ask for access again until August 1987, at which time attorneys were consulted and the present dispute commenced.

Brenda's wish at this time is that Terry have no access to Janie. She bases this on a number of concerns. Brenda cites, first, Terry's history of abusiveness. She worries about Janie witnessing her father's abuse of his wife, and being subject to verbal abuse by Paula. Brenda feels that Terry manipulates, in a controlling manner, the way that Janie feels and see things. For example, she believes that Terry conveys to Janie that her mother doesn't love her. She feels that Terry controls Janie with indirect messages, inducing guilt, for example, about how he would feel if Janie did not visit him. (This is consistent with the way that I saw Terry in the 1983 assessment, where his focus in relation to his children was very much on his own needs).

Brenda worries about Terry's pattern of forming relationships with much younger women, wondering if this will translate to inappropriate behavior in relation to Janie as she gets older.

Brenda is concerned, generally, about the life style to which Terry exposes his daughter, with "partying", drinking, and assaultive behavior.

Brenda feels that the erratic nature of Terry's relationship with Janie has had a negative impact on the youngster. She has seen, she reports, behavioural changes in Janie with her father's appearances and disappearances. When Terry returns after a period of absence, Brenda sees Janie needing an adjustment period, and discipline becomes an issue. For example, Janie resists her mother's direction, saying that she doesn't have to listen. At those times, in Brenda's view, Janie casts her mother as the "bad guy", and her father as the "good guy". At times, coincident with Terry's coming or going, Janie has, for example, if sent to her room, "trashed" her room.

Brenda worries about the very different values to which Janie is exposed at mom's house and dad's house. She feels that in his controlling manner Terry exerts significant negative influence over Janie's values.

I believe that Brenda feels genuinely fearful and intimidated by Terry. She imputes considerable power to Terry in relation to Janie. To some extent, that may be a projection of Brenda's own fear. Without interviewing the father and daughter, it would be difficult to comment on the nature of that interaction. However, as in the past, I found Brenda to be highly child-focused, citing a number of very valid concerns about Terry's relationship with Janie. Brenda displays an awareness of her own reactions to Terry, and believes that she makes an effort to separate her feelings from Janie's feelings about her father. Brenda purports to encourage Janie to express herself openly, and to stress to her that she has a right to her own feelings. She does not feel that Terry offers Janie that sort of encouragement or endorsement. When seen in 1983, with his heavy focus on his own needs, Terry would not, then, have been likely to encourage this sort of individuation. Additional time with Terry would be required to assess whether there has been an improved child-focus.

Janie:

Janie is a likeable, verbal, endearing youngster of almost seven years old. In the context of this assessment, Janie was seen with her mother and mother's partner, and was interviewed individually. When seen with her mother, I did not have a sense *that she was constricted or rehearsed. She seemed comfortable contradicting Brenda.*

Janie stated that she was not very happy about not seeing her father for a long time. She said that she missed him, adding, "I don't want to see him until he stops drinking". On questioning, Janie said that these were her words and her mother's words. Janie indicated that she had witnessed and heard physical violence at her father's home anytime she'd been there. She described her father and Paula fighting, and her father hitting his wife. Janie described herself at sometimes when this was occurring being in bed and trying to sleep but being unable to. She expressed her sadness about the violence. Janie said that she would sometimes ask her father not to fight, and he would say he would try but never did. At other times, Janie described hitting her father on the arm and he would then stop fighting. Janie said that if her father was angry, he would yell at her for no reason. At those times, she would stay out of his way and go to her room.

In Janie's account, her father would drink during all access visits. When drinking, she said he would get mad at Paula and her three year old son Jason for no reason. Janie described Paula trying to call the police when Terry hit her, and Terry not allowing her to do so. Janie expressed the belief that if her father was not drinking he would be nice to Paula, adding that he is not very nice when he drinks. Apparently, Paula left the home during Janie's last March break visit. Janie was, she said "sad and glad". She was sad, she said, because she likes Paula and glad because Paula hurts her feelings by, for example, saying that she is going to hit Janie.

Janie expresses the feeling that hitting is "not very nice". However, she then excuses her father's violence by saying he drinks and doesn't even know what he's doing when he drinks. Already, at six, Janie is learning to rationalize totally unacceptable adult behavior. Like the women in her father's life, Janie has found ways to excuse his abusive behavior.

Janie was very worried about being seen at the Clinic with her father. She stated that if she told the truth in an interview, he would say that she wasn't telling the truth. This certainly fits with Brenda's sense that Janie does not feel that she can be open about her feelings with her father.

Janie did express some positive feelings about access visits. She enjoys time with her older sister Lynn when Lynn is visiting. Janie likes to play with Jason. It sounds, as well, like she attempts to shelter the three year old when Terry and Paula are fighting. Janie enjoys shopping with Paula, and going to the park.

Janie stated that her mom told her when she is older she can make her own decisions about seeing her father. Janie interpreted "older" to mean when she is thirteen.

Janie is a youngster who clearly has an attachment to her father. She expresses a wish to spend time with him, and sadness about the lengthy gaps in access. At the same time, Janie expresses clear distress about drinking and violence to which she has been exposed in the context of time spent with her father. Janie has, both in the past in the context of her parents' relationship, and more recently in terms of Terry's relationship with Paula taken on the onerous and inappropriate role of attempting to intervene when her father is violent with his partner. One gets no sense of stability, security, or predictability in the context of access with her father. Inevitably, access time has been marred by turbulence in her father's life and relationships.

Janie appears very closely bonded to her mother. It is with her mother that her security needs are met. It appears, as well that the emotional upsets which Janie experiences are ventilated with her mother in terms of some intermittent behavioural difficulties. Janie seems to enjoy a positive relationship with Anthony. She seems very comfortable about his participation in her activities and daily routines. Janie related positively some of the activities that she and Anthony enjoy together.

Formulation:

As I have indicated, there are clear limitations in this assessment. I was not able to spend adequate individual time with Terry. I was unable to see Terry with Janie, or with his and Paula's younger child.

In one interview with Terry and Paula, Terry's pattern of projecting blame onto others for his difficulties was still very much apparent. Historical information, and recent criminal charges, provide evidence of continued alcohol abuse and assaultiveness to female partners.

There is enough information available, I believe, to raise considerable concern about the nature of access that should occur between Janie and her father. One needs to address the issue of children being exposed to family violence, in this instance, more specifically, girls being exposed to paternal abuse of female partners. This sort of exposure has been found to impact negatively on girl's self-esteem in terms of the view they form of themselves as females. One needs to be concerned, with Janie, about her inculcating inappropriate values about it being acceptable for females to be physically victimized. One would worry about Janie continuing this pattern into her own relationships, and into the next generation. Janie was already exposed in her first three years of life to abuse and control of her mother by her father, and again in the context of her father's relationship with his wife, Paula. Janie's immediate reaction has been one of distress and upset. In the long term, this may impact in a significant way on her self-esteem as well as her ability to function in male/female relationships. Potentially, it could be very damaging for Janie to continue to be exposed to violence within her family. One can hope that the more positive experience she has enjoyed with her mother and Anthony, and her mother's efforts to teach her more appropriate values, will mitigate against the negative exposure that Janie has had.

I would be concerned about Terry's dysfunctional manner of relating to women being projected onto Janie when she becomes an adolescent and is less amenable to control.

Given Terry's chronic alcohol abuse, and assaultive behavior, the stability and predictability of an access situation could not help but be seriously undermined.

As stated in the introductory section of this report, I feel unable, given the limitations of the assessment, to make recommendations about whether access between Janie and her father should occur. I feel enough concern based on the information available, to recommend, at the least, some restrictions in access that might be ordered. If Terry and Paula reconcile, I would recommend that access not take place in their home. Rather, if access is ordered, I would see it taking the form of day visits in Kingston. If Terry and Paula do not reconcile, but Terry enters a new relationship, the nature of that relationship would need to be carefully examined. If access is ordered, given Brenda's fearful reaction to Terry, I would not see the utility in de-stabilizing the custodial situation by imposing a condition that father pick the child up at her home. There would need to be a neutral drop-off and pick-up location. Access visits would need to be structured to ensure that father not consume alcohol. This might for example, take the form of an order for supervised antabuse to precede access visits.

In summary, in order to make a clear recommendation about whether access should occur would require additional interviews with Terry and interview time with Terry and Janie. At this point, I have a number of concerns which I feel would justify, at the least, restrictions in any access situation that might take place. These restrictions would be geared towards preventing continued exposure for Janie to violent family situations and to her father's alcohol abuse.

Hoping that this report serves as useful to the parties and the court, I remain,

Yours truly,

Family Court Clinic

Upon the completion of the new assessment the judge stated his concern that a denial of access can cause children to fantasize about the missing parent. He did, however, agree that Janie should not be exposed to ongoing violence and decided to order one hour of supervised access per month. Terry only showed up about twice at the court house for his supervised visit, then he left Kingston and returned to Ottawa. While it seemed that Terry was now out of our lives, I continued to look over my shoulder for the next few years. But he never bothered us again.

During these early years Jane was my best and closest friend. She was glad that I was moving forward and offered encouragement at every opportunity. I was suddenly pretty protected, compared to my previous life.

It was hard to make the switch from being constantly abused and living in terror to a life where things were calm and reasonable all the time. Sometimes this change alone was very confusing and hard to deal with as the roller coaster no longer existed. While I can't say I missed the roller coaster, I can say it was not an easy transition.

After getting my first job and working for a number of months I had the opportunity to enrol in the Futures program. This was a year-long government funded program that gave youth the chance to upgrade their education and provided job placements. I graduated from this program and was hired back to tutor math for other students in the program. During this time my self-esteem was growing, and I was able to be around other people with no jealous rages to deal with.

I started to entertain the idea of going to college, and Anthony along with those around me were very supportive. After looking at the programs offered, I knew it would be computers or accounting. I really liked math and accounting so I decided that I would enrol in the three-year accounting program.

This was a very scary time for me, as I had lived all my life day to day. Each day I got up, I was happy to be free and to have Anthony and Janie, but I was also always looking over my shoulder. Life is good when you are able to view each day as a gift. The idea of a three year commitment to school scared me very much. I decided to enrol and take it one day at a time. I would do my best, but I wouldn't make a promise that I would stay the full three years. This rationalization made it easier for me to enrol.

In September 1986 I began a three-year accounting program. I did struggle with a couple of classes, and felt I shouldn't have to do some of the required things, such as group projects and public presentations. I went away and thought about it deciding that although I didn't want to do those things if they were requirements for the diploma that I did want, I would do them. My education went fine after I adopted that attitude.

In fact, I was hooked by the end of the first semester. I loved school. I was smart and I had proof with the great marks I was getting. This had to be one of the biggest self-esteem boosters I had in my life. Although I now had some people telling me I was capable, it was different to have tests that proved I was smart. I graduated with distinction, in the top of my class.

After my first semester of school I started encouraging Anthony to go back to school. He had always been good with electronics and he decided to return to school and take the Electronics Technician program. Our programs overlapped and although Anthony went to school in the summer he was there with me for my second year. We made some friends and enjoyed having lunch together.

By the time Anthony started school we had been together for three years and we started talking about having a baby. I explained that I had a tubal ligation when I was 16 and could not have any more children. Anthony said he was fine with not having any children, but when I asked him how many he would like if it was possible, he surprised me by claiming he would like a dozen. I started talking to doctors to see if there was any way to have a child.

I had several bad experiences with doctors, but I persisted and finally found one who didn't treat me like I was worthless, and who gave me a referral to a specialist in Kingston. After medical tests for both myself and Anthony, I was a candidate for surgery. They phoned in early 1987 to say I had an appointment for surgery in March. Considering the school semester was over in May, I postponed the reversal surgery until then.

After the surgery the doctor made no promises as I only had the one tube, but he was optimistic that the surgery had been a success. They did suggest that if the surgery was not successful in vitro fertilization would be the next option.

While we had fun trying for a baby, it wasn't until March of 1988 that we were finally successful. Anthony was graduating in the spring of 1988. He took a summer job as an electrician on the military base in Kingston, and in the fall of 1988, just after the birth of Amanda, he was offered a permanent position with his current company.

While we were both excited about the pending arrival of our new baby, I found it hard to believe. Life was just too good, and I couldn't believe it would last. I had nightmares that something would happen to our baby before her arrival. Like she had disappeared, or never really existed in the first place. It wasn't until she actually arrived that I could believe it was all real. Amanda was born in the middle of my fifth semester and I didn't miss a beat, I completed my semester and my year to graduate.

She was the most beautiful baby and I felt so blessed to have had the two most beautiful children in the world. Janie was very excited by the birth of her new sister and was organizing a visit for her whole class by the time Anthony got to pick her up at the end of the day and bring her to the hospital.

After graduation I got a full time job as an accountant for a local franchise company. This was a very stressful job due to lack of money and constant calls from creditors. After a couple of years I was thinking, "Man, I can't do this for 40 more years."

For the next couple of years we tried for a third child, and watched Amanda grow and blossom, she was perfect in every way. You could take her anywhere and she would sit and visit, or eat, she never complained and was always happy. Even the baby sitter said she was the perfect child.

Despite all this I was starting to have some depressing thoughts, starting to feel overwhelmed. Sometimes I just felt like I had cheated, that I didn't deserve what I had, and at any time it could be taken away from me. Just as my depression started to take hold, we found out I was pregnant with our third child.

Although we had been trying for a while, when I talked to the doctor he felt I would probably require additional surgery to have another child. We had decided we were very fortunate to have two children and I didn't want to undergo any additional major surgery.

We were very happy about the birth of our third child, Ashley. She was also the most beautiful baby in the world. However, at this time postpartum depression set in for me and went undiagnosed until a much later date. I had a hard time thinking of anything other than how much more laundry there would be to do.

My depression worsened until it reached a point where I was no longer able to work. I was fortunate enough to be able to apply for Canada Pension Plan disability benefits (CPP).

DEALING WITH THE PAST, WELCOMING THE FUTURE

After purchasing our first home and settling in with the children, the past began to catch up with me. I now had three young children to raise and protect. It seemed a daunting task for just two parents. Along with my depression came huge anxiety attacks. I was scared that at any moment I would wake up and everyone I loved would be gone. I felt worthless, and worst of all I felt like I had cheated fate. In my mind, I didn't deserve a wonderful husband and three beautiful daughters and it was just a matter of time before they were gone. Waiting for the moment when I lost it all was slowly driving me crazy.

I had this long list of rules about the right and wrong way to do everything, how to be a good wife, a good mother, and a good person. These rules became so unreasonable I couldn't possibly follow them all, and this made me even more depressed. The biggest problem with the rules I had for being the perfect mother, the perfect wife, the perfect neighbour, and the perfect friend was that I was hugely disappointed when everyone else failed to follow my rules. My self-esteem, which had come a long way since my early days with Anthony, was almost non-existent once again.

I had literally stopped participating in life. I started taking anti-depressants and lost two years to Prozac. I started going to counselling and while I am sure my counsellor didn't think I was making any progress, it would all come together at a later date. I attended counselling regularly for a number of years, and when I wasn't making any changes in my life, I could say that at least I was trying. It was important for me to have the knowledge that at least I was trying to do something about it.

Counselling began with talking about my past, a past I had kept very compartmentalized as a coping mechanism. I had viewed the events in my childhood each as an isolated event. Upon spending some time talking about the past it allowed me to put it all together like a big puzzle. Suddenly it was one big unpleasant picture, and it took me some time to come to terms with this. In some ways it was like being traumatized all over again.

I had never put together how abused I had been and suddenly seeing it as one big picture, made me very angry. I was angry at a world that could let such things happen to children. I was very angry at Terry for all he had also taken away from me.

I was diagnosed with post-traumatic stress disorder, clinical depression, and chronic fatigue syndrome. There were times when these diagnoses seemed like a cop out, as none of these three conditions have any clear evidence to support them. While there was no doubt that I was depressed, I often wrestled with the chronic fatigue syndrome. Sometimes I felt like I had it, and other times I felt like no one knew what was wrong. I received CPP disability benefits based on the chronic fatigue syndrome. The diagnosis was based on my elevated white blood cell count. This meant I was exhausted at all times because my immune system was continually working in overdrive to fight off any virus.

During my years of counselling, I slowly began dealing with the past. Periodically I had to take Ashley with me. The counsellor always mentioned how good I was with her. I was good at playing with the kids and entertaining them. I knew what they liked, what would keep them busy, and what would catch their attention. I loved to see them smile and sometimes that is what kept me going for one more day.

During the Prozac years I would occasionally forget to pick up the kids from school, until either the school called or the kids themselves called. I would tell Janie to wait after school and I would pick her up and then by the end of the day I would forget. Anthony started keeping a calendar for me and would remind me each morning where I was going and what appointments I had.

I was also suffering from anxiety attacks on a regular basis. It got to the point where I felt like I couldn't continue. I had difficulty leaving the house for any period of time; fear would creep in and cripple me. While I was often able to recognize that the fear was unreasonable or out of proportion, I wasn't able to do more than hang on and pray for it to end. If we went out for dinner I could last about an hour and then would stand up and announce I was going home and anyone coming needed to head to the car.

I had at this time filed an application with the Criminal Injuries Compensation Board (CICB). Who requested that I file a police report. I thought about this, and how filing the report would require documenting and reliving the past, but decided to go ahead and file the report. However, after an officer talked to my mother she phoned screaming at me. I explained that the CICB had requested I file the report. I tried to explain to her that it seemed that no one cared about me as a child. She told me that no one gave a shit about me then, and no one gave a shit about me now either. Although this statement from my mother should not have come as any surprise, it was devastating. Maybe I had been hoping all these years that my childhood feelings hadn't really been true.

My mother wasted no time in calling the officer back to tell her that I was only filing the complaint to receive money. The officer called me after taking my mother's statement and said in view of my mother's statement she would be unable to continue with the investigation. Criminal Injuries decided there was not enough evidence to process my complaint.

As a child and into adulthood, I had never believed that I would live past 40, and I began to realize I needed to make preparations now. I had always believed that if your morning goes bad it will affect your whole day, and I had a rule that I didn't fight or argue with anyone in the morning. I started to think, if this is true, could it be that if you leave this life miserable you start your next life miserable? Since I am not a big believer in life after death or even God for that matter, I had to give this some thought. I decided that while I wasn't sure if there is a life after death, I sure didn't want to be wrong in the process. I wanted to enjoy the five years I hoped I had left, or at least make sure my kids enjoyed them.

With years of counselling and a desire to be happy, I reached a turning point. Slowly I started to get better. At first, I had some good days here and there. I started teaching part time at the college, and I loved having the students and feeling like I was making a contribution to their lives. We also got a Jack Russell puppy. The nice thing about a dog is it loves you unconditionally. This made me recognize that I had made up so many rules, that I could not possibly succeed in following them all. My guess is that because I lacked the experience and social guides in my life, I made up rules as I went along - rules on how to be the perfect mother, wife, or friend. Slowly I started to relax the rules; counselling helped me realize that the rules were too black and white, and that sometimes life has grey areas. As I started to relax the rules, I also began to lighten up on myself.

Throughout this rough time in my life, Jane was my rock. She listened to me when I was sure no one else would have wanted to; she offered positive suggestions and kept redirecting me. I am sure that her non-judgmental support was crucial to my recovery.

In my depression, I was also convinced that Anthony didn't really love me. He might believe he did, but he couldn't really because I was undeserving. Jane pointed out that if he thought he loved me, then he loved me; since it was about his perception, not just mine. I gave this some thought and was able to understand and finally accept the fact that my husband did actually love me. That helped relieve a lot of my fear and anxiety.

As it turns out, Anthony loved me very much and wanted to help me move forward and feel better. I started confiding in Anthony and had someone to talk with during these anxiety attacks. Progress was slow here because it was about trusting and letting another person in. While we had been together for quite some time, I don't think I had ever let him in. This was a turning point in my healing. As I had worked so hard to suffer alone, letting someone else in was a big breakthrough and a positive move.

I won tickets to an Amanda Marshall concert and while I wasn't very familiar with her work, I was excited to win the tickets and so we travelled to Ottawa to see her. When she came out on stage her opening song was "I Believe In You" and I remember being so moved by that song all I could do was sit and cry.

I still suffered anxiety attacks but they were slowly diminishing. Recovery was a long process, and I had to keep reminding myself that I didn't get sick quickly either. Once I got off the anti-depressants and started working I started the long journey to recovery. While psycho-active drugs can be an important part of recovery, they alone were not the answer for me. Rather, or in addition to, it is a matter of processing life's events and finding a way of putting it all in perspective so that future day-to-day living allows you to move forward positively.

Dealing with the past, however you decide to do it, is the best way to move forward. I had to acknowledge the past instead of continuing to spend time trying to forget, or pretend it never happened. Once I acknowledged the past, then I had to allow myself time to grieve. I needed to grieve for all that had been taken away from me, for all that could have been if I had been born into better circumstances. I was also sad and angry because I had no say in the decisions affecting my early life.

After moving through the grieving process I had to recognize that very little of my past was my fault. I realized in my case it is best to put the past in the past, and accomplished this by processing and accepting it. This of course took time, and in the process I also had to try to let the guilt go as well.

Years of guilt had kept me from moving forward, as I believe guilt can suppress anger. Once I was able to address the anger and put these events in the past I was able to look ahead and start to change how I thought and processed future events. I realize this sounds like a simple process, however it took me years of counselling to move through this process.

I continued teaching part time and this was important for my self-esteem. I am a big believer in education and the benefit it provides. An education gives everyone the opportunity and tools to control their lives. Outside of my work life, I enjoyed gardening and found the benefits to be huge, because while working in my garden I could focus on only one task at a time, methodically. It also taught me patience as sometimes when I moved plants from one to location to another I would have to wait a whole year to see the results. Gardening provided a creative outlet, which I believe is important for everyone, regardless of how much creative ability we feel we have. Gardening led to a pond, as the children had pet turtles, which were getting too big to keep in an aquarium. From the pond I soon discovered my love of turtles, frogs, butterflies and all the creatures that nature brought my way.

I eventually felt able to take a part-time job where I worked 15 hours a week. This was overwhelming at first, and meant I had to leave the house for periods longer than an hour. I slowly adjusted and stayed at this job for three years while I continued to improve.

I then accepted a full-time job at a non-profit organization that provides services for vulnerable people in our community. While I felt this was a good fit for me, I was scared to death. It had been 11 years since I had worked full time, and I wasn't sure if I could do it, or for how long. Again I decided to take it one day at a time - small steps eventually make up an entire journey.

While working part time, my goal had been to return to work full time. I have now been at my full time job for over seven years and continue to teach at the local college. I still love the students, and the feeling that I am giving something back. Over the years I have had some wonderful comments from the students. And I have been surprised by my children as well. It is nice to know that they love me and think highly of me.

I think we do not know the true extent of our abilities until we are put to the test. Through my experiences, the best advice I can offer for dealing with anything is this: when faced with a challenge, it is OK to break it down into workable pieces; we don't have to solve the whole problem all at once.

I can truly say I am happy, probably the happiest I have ever been. It is genuine and not just about being alive today. I no longer feel like I cheated fate, but rather that I have worked very hard to achieve what I have and therefore I deserve it. I could have taken many different paths but I kept focused on straight ahead, even though there were times when I was sure I was following a dead end. I work hard at being positive every day, as being negative is sometimes too easy.

It feels good to be home and to have a family that I love and that loves me in return. That is the best gift anyone could have. As a bonus, I get to influence the lives of young people and hopefully share my passion for education; it is the single greatest thing that someone can do for themselves.

In closing I would like to say that I was very fortunate to be touched and influenced by many people, some for a short time such as Shelly, some for a longer time, such as the Lake's and of course some for a lifetime like Jane, Daniel, and my husband, Anthony.

While I know that Jane would never take credit for any of it, I have to say that I do not have the words to truly express her importance in my life, and no doubt many other lives. She gave me hope when I didn't see any, she gave me optimism when I was negative, but most importantly she gave me the love of a mother - something I hadn't experienced until I met Jane. I hope I have expressed my feelings of her importance in my life, and the gratitude I feel for having her continue to be part of my life.

I am successful and happy beyond what my childhood self ever imagined; I have a college degree, a university degree, a successful career in accounting and teaching. As I prepare to publish this book I am overcome with the same childhood guilt, that somehow I am sharing secrets that shouldn't be told. I worry about how co-worker's will see me if they should read this. Then I remind myself, I didn't do anything wrong, I have nothing to feel ashamed about, I was a victim of circumstances beyond my control, there is nothing to feel guilty or ashamed of.

One of the best rewards was hearing my daughter say that when people ask who her role model or her hero is, she says it's her mom.

WHERE ARE THEY NOW

Readers of earlier editions often asked what happened to some of the people in my story, so I will share the ones I know.

Jane is now retired and still an important part of my life. She still helps a lot of people, with her positive and encouraging ways.

Daniel is happily married and once again an important part of my life.

Lynn passed away shortly after her 21st birthday, due to complications with her illness.

Shelly, I just found out passed away 2 years ago.

Baby sister has two children, but custody of neither. I don't see much of her. This is a direct result of fetal alcohol syndrome.

Janie is married to a wonderful man and has one child, my handsome grandson. She works as a PSW in a northern community.

Amanda is a manager and a chemical engineer. She has lived and worked all over Canada. Currently she resides in BC.

Ashley, the youngest is busy finding herself and discovering her passions.

Anthony, after a long career, plans to retire this spring. I am excited to enter this new stage of our lives together.

<u>EPILOGUE</u>

Over the years I have been asked, "What was it that enabled you to overcome the past?" As you can see from the book, there is no one-sentence answer to that question. For me it was primarily a series of fortunate occurrences that involved a number of very caring people before I was able to find my way.

Daniel of course was a huge influence on me at a very young age. Looking back, my experience with him taught me there were exceptions, not all men were bad. It is probably because of Daniel's early love and support that I was able to establish a healthy relationship with my husband.

As a child I knew that I didn't belong where I was, or at least I believed that to be true. I fantasized as a child that my 'dad' was going to come save me, when he found out about me.

Despite some of the horrible experiences I had in some foster homes, there were some foster parents who really tried to positively influence my life. I thank them.

And then of course, there is Jane. I was very fortunate to have her come into my life and to hang in with me for the long haul. She helped me develop the trust and people attachments that allowed me to move forward. I'm still in touch with her today.

Years of counselling with a truly amazing woman, also helped me let the past go and assisted me with envisioning a new future. A future that involved changing my thought patterns from negative to positive. Something I still work on every day.

And finally, a loving husband. Through it all I have always been able to count on him. I'm very grateful.

I realize that I have personalized my response to the initial question within the context of my story. But allow me to approach this in slightly more generic terms. Knowing what I know now, here are the steps that I feel are necessary to overcome being a victim of child abuse.

First, you need to acknowledge the past abuse. This may require professional help, to help cope with the feelings of guilt, anger and possibly depression. It is important to realize that you didn't do anything wrong, it wasn't your fault! I realized how important this was after spending years trying to block or bury the past only to have it control my future. In addition, it is necessary in order to start changing the negative thoughts about yourself that guilt, anger, and depression have created. You were a victim, but now you are a survivor.

Second, it is OK to be angry with the person who hurt you. Actually it is important to be angry. Often this anger has been directed internally and it needs to be directed externally. Once I was able to redirect this anger I was also able to start thinking more positively about myself. This will allow you to continue the process of leaving the past behind. During this time you need to keep working on changing thoughts of yourself from negative into positive. It takes practice, but it is critical to allowing you to envision a new future.

Third, start visualizing your future. Think of the many people you have come in contact with in your life. What did you like about them or their lives, what did you find calming about them? For some this may be the only basis available to visualize the life they would like to have. While the life you would like may be very different from where you are now, it is a process of small steps. When you can start to visualize the life you deserve, break it down into small steps and goals. Remember you do deserve the life you want. 'Life is a journey' as the saying goes, and yours is just beginning.

Finally, keep focused on the small goals. It is the series of small goals that make up the larger goals. If you see yourself in a new career, enroll in just one course to determine if you enjoy it. Or maybe you could do some volunteer work in that field. Think about things that interest you such as art, gardening, advocating for others. Then take a class or join a group. As you plan and achieve small goals, remember you are moving from survivor to victor.

But although I do not profess to be an expert, these steps represent a summary of what worked for me. It is never a quick or easy journey for victims of abuse. These steps can help as they represent an outline of what moved me along from victim to survivor, and ultimately made me into a victor.

Photo Courtesy of Darren Kelly- www.dbkcreative.com

ABOUT THE AUTHOR

Brenda Secor works as a financial manager for a non-profit community service agency. She is also an accounting professor at a local community college where she shares her passion for life-long learning. She currently lives in south-eastern Ontario with her husband, Anthony and her Jack Russell Terrier, Sally. She has three adult daughters.

Brenda is available for public speaking and lecturing at colleges and universities whose programs focus on child welfare. She can be reached through her website: www.findingjane.ca

A portion of the proceeds from the sale of this book will go to helping youth in the Kingston Community.

If you would like to make a donation directly to youth in need, please go to the following website: www.kingstonhomebase.ca

CPSIA information can be obtained at www.ICGtesting.com
Printed in the USA
LVOW04s2137250515

439714LV00023B/674/P

9 780991 823604